C000182979

MINDCRAFTING

MINDCRAFTING

How to Mentor Your Ageing Mind

Dr Declan Lyons

With contributions from Dr Jennifer Keane,
Dr Molly Bredin and Dr Ailbhe Doherty

BEEHIVE

Published 2022 by
Beehive Books
7–8 Lower Abbey Street
Dublin 1
info@beehivebooks.ie
www.beehivebooks.ie

Beehive Books is an imprint of Veritas Publications

Copyright © Dr Declan Lyons, 2022

ISBN: 978 1 80097 013 7

10 9 8 7 6 5 4 3 2 1

The material in this publication is protected by copyright law. Except as may be permitted by law, no part of the material may be reproduced (including by storage in a retrieval system) or transmitted in any form or by any means, adapted, rented or lent without the written permission of the copyright owners. Applications for permissions should be addressed to the publisher.

A catalogue record for this book is available from the British Library.

Designed and typeset by Padraig McCormack, Beehive Books
Printed in the Republic of Ireland by SPRINT-print Ltd, Dublin

Beehive books are printed on paper made from the wood pulp of managed forests. For every tree felled, at least one tree is planted, thereby renewing natural resources.

To Maria, Julie and Evan who have patiently waited for my return to the domestic taxi rank.

To all those longevity-minded senior citizens who continue to inspire, enthuse and lead by devoting their lives to the service of others.

Contents

Acknowledgements

My thanks to all the people whom I have had the privilege to treat over the years, who have given me great insight into the challenges and opportunities associated with growing older. My colleagues at St Patrick's Mental Health Services, who form the multidisciplinary team caring for older people with mental health challenges, are dedicated experts in their field, yet by understanding the struggles and the hopes of patients we care for, we gain enormous inspiration and motivation to continue with and, as much as possible, to perfect our work.

My gratitude to my colleagues and chapter contributors, Drs Jennifer Keane, Molly Bredin and Ailbhe Doherty. By their hard work, all have contributed to making Vanessa ward at St Patrick's Hospital a holistic haven of mental health care.

I wish to acknowledge Joe Griffin and Ivan Tyrrell, founders of the Human Givens approach to understanding emotional and psychological difficulties that forms the basis of my description of the crucial needs of older people, which are highlighted in this book. Denise Winn of the Human Givens College provided invaluable advice about the structure and layout of the initial draft of this work.

I greatly appreciated the advice and input of the staff from Veritas who were all incredibly supportive, patient and professional, particularly Síne Quinn, Mags Gargan, David Macken, Denise Murphy, Tony Moroney, Aidan Chester and

Daragh Reddin. I wish their new imprint Beehive Books every success in the non-fiction and children's books market.

I very much appreciate the endorsements from Dr Claire Hayes, Joe Griffin and Dr Harry Barry, who are all notable authors in the field of mental health. Your inboxes are perpetually full, yet you took time out to scan my offerings. Your collective influence goes beyond the plaudits you have each received for your own works, and your mentorship and encouragement has inspired me in many ways.

On behalf of the authors, our greatest debt undoubtedly goes to our families (in my case especially to Maria) who have tolerated the time taken to write this book, as well as the inevitable angst a project like this generates.

I hope this book showcases the numerous possibilities as well as the potential pitfalls associated with old age. I have been very privileged to work in a job where each day is guaranteed to be different to the last and where dullness is dispelled by the variety of humbling encounters that those of us working in mental health have with our patients, each and every day.

Introduction

Longevity has added twenty-five years to our life expectancy over the last century – we now survive the equivalent of a whole new adult lifetime longer than our great-grandparents. This presents enormous opportunities to grow and thrive during this period in our lives, especially if life pressures such as paying off a mortgage have eased or goals for childrearing have been achieved. Perhaps the daily grind associated with a long commute or a tedious job is finally over. So what happens next?

It is undeniable that society pays more attention to younger people in their struggle to navigate life's transitions than to older people, who arguably have to cope with a greater number of demarcation points in their lives. The major changes and challenges faced by seniors are, in many ways, bigger than those of younger people and some, such as the greater likelihood of illness and bereavement, are outside the direct control of the individual.

Career guidance counselling has become a new subspecialty in the education system of many countries, yet no direct parallel exists for older people. Many companies and organisations pay only lip service to the notion of retirement planning, frequently outsourcing these 'softer skills' rather than providing this support within their own human resources departments, where staff may know the potential retirees personally and have ideas for how their skill sets could most satisfyingly be deployed in a post-work setting. Very few, if any, organisations have a retirement counsellor employed within their management structures. University faculties rarely set out to attract older students and those that develop courses in life skills for seniors are thin on the ground.

While many of the milestones of human development in adulthood, such as cohabitation and marriage or homeownership can be deferred, avoided or enacted at any stage of the life cycle, older people may find themselves being shoved from one crossroads to the next and having to deal with significant stresses simultaneously. Some of the many challenges that may be faced include:

- Retirement (voluntary or involuntary)
- Adult children leaving the family home
- Financial pressures
- Health challenges and multiple bereavements
- Managing new technology
- Greater physical dependency and emerging needs in executing daily living skills
- Difficulty getting around, whether because of reduced mobility or poor public transport
- Changes in memory and cognitive function
- Greater stereotyping and marginalisation than for other groups in society
- Overt and covert age discrimination or restrictions
- Grandparenting and acquisition of a new skill set in this area
- Changes in sensory abilities, particularly vision and hearing
- Need to support adult children
- Managing free time effectively post work
- Changing requirements in terms of living arrangements and associated stresses.

I can't stress enough, however, that it is impossible to generalise about older people. They are not a single homogenous group. Indeed, as a segment of society, older people are incredibly varied, and this variation increases, not decreases, as we add to our years. Many people of 65 may, for instance, be closer to middle age in their own mindsets, whereas others may have very different self-perceptions.

Society makes many assumptions about people when they enter the 'third age' of their lives. Upon acquiring that pension or free travel pass or having been expelled from the workplace, older people may suddenly find themselves dismissed and ignored or at the receiving end of crude humour and stereotyping. All that expertise, emotional maturity and refined brainpower risks being neutralised by a society that chooses to push away all signs of encroaching mortality through use of grim-sounding labels such as 'geriatric' and 'senile'. Little wonder that many older people may withdraw or surrender and passively accept the norms imposed by others, succumbing albeit reluctantly to expecting nothing more for themselves than bridge, bingo and stamp collecting – perfectly enjoyable activities in themselves but not necessarily the be-all and end-all of a person's ambition.

Older people are too often made convenient scapegoats for many of society's ills and failings, suffering the ignominy of being called 'bed blockers' in our overcrowded hospitals or 'home blockers' because they continue to live in a familiar family home in the midst of a housing crisis. Or, as a social group, they may be perceived as a drain on society's resources because they are provided with pensions and other benefits. Is it any wonder many older people lower their expectations of themselves, disengage and become depressed, living out psychologically impoverished lives amidst a society that seems mesmerised by youth? Each generation seems to repeat the same mistakes, failing to recognise the value and reap the rewards of the longevity dividend brought about through increased life expectancy.

Later life needs, quite simply, to take an upward shift in status as well as years. As someone who has worked exclusively with older patients in medicine and psychiatry for twenty-five years, I have come to admire older people for their resilience, fortitude and determination to get on with the business of daily life without being a burden on anyone else, despite some developing illnesses such as dementia, severe depression or chronic physical illnesses. I hold in awe those who ignore social constructs about what older people should or should not be engaged with and, whilst being neither outrageous nor controversial, simply carry on doing or building on what they've always done while remaining receptive to new experiences and challenges.

Frank Lloyd Wright, the accomplished American architect, began work on the futuristic Guggenheim Museum in New York at the age of 76, a project he continued to work on until his death at the age of 91. Another inspirational senior citizen of recent times who began a late blossoming career was the novelist Mary Wesley, who had her first book published at the age of 71 and continued to publish until the age of 84. Many people now seek to reinvent themselves after retirement and launch a second career that can represent the pinnacle of earlier, albeit postponed, personal ambition.

Throughout my career I have practised holistically, seeing the older person as a repository of wisdom, ability, talent and experience. Whilst mental health challenges may sometimes dim these attributes temporarily, it is up to professionals, such as myself, to make sure the person's core skills and talents are not extinguished and can form the basis of recovery and restoration of functioning.

The framework for understanding human behaviour, which is provided by an awareness of the necessity for human beings to fulfil innate emotional and psychological needs, forms the basis of my day-to-day clinical interactions as a consultant psychiatrist with a specialist interest in the mental health of older people. I shall refer throughout this book to this premise as a set of organising ideas termed the Human Givens,[1] and explain how it has particular relevance for older people – both those who want to take full advantage of the opportunities still open to them and also those who find themselves struggling with mental health difficulties or other constraints. I strongly endorse the view that – irrespective of any underlying problem or diagnosis – if emotional and psychological needs are met in a balanced way, mental health difficulties at any age are significantly reduced.

I believe that these principles apply not just to individuals but also to communities, wider society and humankind as a whole, and that the best way to overcome increasing levels of psychological dysfunction in society is to actively deploy our innate resources to meet our universal emotional needs healthily and sustainably. The framework of needs and resource awareness is thus the basis for flourishing in later years.

A word about pronouns: As I write, I envisage you the reader as someone of older age or someone who cares about someone older. However, older age or later life, as I point out, can span a great many years – more, perhaps, than any of the other life stages. As not everything I have to say will apply to every reader at all times, I have chosen to refer sometimes to 'you', sometimes to 'us' and sometimes to 'them' to cover this huge potential variability in readership.

---

1   Joe Griffin and Ivan Tyrrell, *Human Givens: The New Approach to Emotional Health and Clear Thinking,* East Sussex: HG Publishing, 2003.

PART I
Perspectives on later life

There may be many reasons why a book on ageing issues piques someone's interest. Perhaps what we term the 'third age' or 'old age' is looming for you over the horizon (whatever that means – they keep moving the goalposts, with 50, then 60, then 70 being the new 40) and you want to stay active, energetic and engaged with life.

Or perhaps you are already in 'older age' and want to make the most of new free time in retirement, if the mortgage has been paid off, the children are reared and you have a comfortable income. Or perhaps you are one of those many older people struggling to make ends meet, still paying rent or a mortgage, trying to help out offspring with their own children or facing life alone for the first time after the loss of a much-loved partner. Perhaps you are thinking ahead to the health problems that you imagine are virtually inevitable in old age (they are not) and this can be a source of loss and even depression for many.

Maybe younger relatives are pressuring you to live and behave in ways that *they* think are appropriate, rather than what *you* think are desirable. Or perhaps you *are* that younger relative and you want to be able to understand older age better and help someone you love to live it as best they can.

Whatever your circumstances, this book will open your eyes to a lot of ideas and understandings that will completely change your perspective of the latter part of life.

When does 'later life' start?

It must be one of life's unspoken ambitions that we all wish to live a full, long and complete life. Yet, as we approach chronological milestones, namely significant birthdays such as a sixtieth or seventieth (which actually indicate that our aspirations are being realised), many of us panic and bemoan the passing years, looking to the future with anxiety and trepidation. Some may increasingly wonder if what they have done with their time on earth bears any significance and are highly conscious that they have fewer years ahead of them than they might wish for.

We may not have realised it but the themes of our earlier years were largely about establishing territory, regard and affection. Later life, though, is about laying down our legacy and finding and building meaning into life as we look backwards to make sense of it all – and, more importantly, try to look ahead with expectation and hope. The days when retirement was perceived as the tail end of life are well and truly over, but the abruptness of leaving full-time work, having sailed along through seemingly full and endless middle years, can come as a shock to many. If a job or a role provided you with purpose, authority and status, and almost literally 'minded you' for forty hours a week, what or who will do the minding now? Retirement and the dawning of the 'third phase of life' or 'old age' is, therefore, a clarion call to review and take stock in relation to those bigger questions now demanding answers. So it is common to ask 'Who am I now? Can I still make a difference? How do I redefine myself, and what's the first step?'

When exactly old age or later life begins is very much open to speculation. We may have wilfully postponed gracefully accepting the impact of 'cumulative chronological shortcomings' or TMB (too many birthdays) syndrome for many years, but how much longer can we cling on to this state of denial? When do we finally have to bow to the inevitable reality that we have reached old age? (Many of us resolutely cling to the belief that an older person is always someone five years older than we are!) And are our ideas out of date?

We have traditionally thought of the mid sixties as the milestone marking entitlement to certain benefits or privileges, such as a state or occupational pension or a free travel pass, but the majority of people are still highly active at that age now. Admittance to specialist hospital medical services starts sometimes at 65 and sometimes at 70, indicating that the start of later life or the 'third age' is quite arbitrary, depending on what is being provided.

'Old age' is not a definite biological state, as any and every entry point denoted as its 'official start' varies culturally and historically. The United Nations has stated that being over 65 counts as being old in a developed country, yet an African research study I came across set 55 as the beginning of old age.

To some extent the answer to the question 'When does old age begin?' depends on the age of the person answering the question and their perceptions. In a US survey of almost three thousand adults, carried out in 2009, people under 30 believed that old age 'strikes' before the average person turns 60, whereas middle-aged respondents said that old age begins at 70, and adults aged 65 or older put the threshold closer to 74. Gender seems to play a part in our outlook, too, with women defining a person as old at age 70, while men believe that 66 counts as being old. The overall consensus from this widely reported research was that 68 indicated the start of the golden years. Yet the old cliché that you're as old as you feel seems to ring true from this sample, as 60 per cent of adults aged 65 and older stated that they felt younger than their actual age.[1]

The number of older people is rapidly increasing around the world, and that is irrespective of where we live. This is primarily due to the post-World War II baby boom and to increases in the standards of healthcare, hygiene and housing. Falling fertility rates also mean that older people make up a greater proportion of the population than ever before in human history. Data from the United Nations in 2017 estimate that there were approximately 962 million people aged 60 and over in the world, comprising 13 per cent of the global population. That number is projected to be 1.4 billion by 2030 (out of a total population of 8.6 billion people of all ages) and 2.1 billion by 2050 (out of a projected total population of 9.8 billion), even potentially rising to the astounding figure of 3.1 billion by 2100.[2] Such ever-increasing numbers of older people living in all societies on earth only serve to confirm that variety and diversity are likely to characterise older people as a group.

Here is some more good news. Even if people get broadly categorised as having reached old age once they are in their late sixties, those aged between 65 and 68 are in fact

---

1   Paul Taylor et al., *Growing Old in America: Expectations vs. Reality*, Washington DC: Pew Research Center, 2009.
2   United Nations Department of Economic and Social Affairs, Population Division, *World Population Prospects: The 2017 Revision, Key Findings and Advance Tables*, New York: United Nations, 2017, p. 17.

psychologically and biologically much closer to middle age. Some of us may enjoy vitality, energy and excellent health right up to the end of our lifespan, whilst others, through no fault of their own, have very different experiences, sadly including illness, disability, dementia and premature death. In fact, the variety between individuals increases, not decreases, as we age – although, of course, those in their eighties may have very different needs and abilities from before. So, rather than lumping together all people over 65 as old, some academics who study the concerns of older people prefer to define sub-groups of older age, which more accurately portrays the life changes that become significant as we accumulate years. You may belong, therefore, to the young-old category (65 to 74 years); to the middle-old (75 to 84); or oldest-old category (85 plus), with the experiences and challenges faced by each often being markedly different.

What else may signal the start of later life?

If you are approaching or already in older age, whichever way you define it, you may feel that this stage in life is more than just a chronological event – what about other life dimensions in the more social and/or psychological realms, which can have a big impact in terms of how you see yourself? How do you respond to the following?

Do you feel you must be old when …
- you become a grandparent?
- you begin to do less work than before?
- you experience age discrimination and rejection whilst applying for a job?
- you struggle to get to grips with a new computer system?
- your work colleagues take lunch breaks and don't bother to invite you?

- work colleagues no longer seek your counsel when it comes to handling challenging aspects of the job?
- your adult children leave the family nest?
- you are faced with a personal health crisis, or the loss of a loved one, or of any meaningful relationship which hitherto buffered many life changes?
- strangers offer spontaneous kindness or respect, such as giving up a seat on a bus?

Did you find yourself saying yes to any of the above?

Taking stock

In many ways, by looking after ourselves reasonably well, we can dupe ourselves into believing that we are stalling even the external signs of ageing. Indeed, you may positively glow with greater security, greater decisiveness and broadmindedness, despite the nagging awareness that the future is no longer as spacious as it once was. This is the gift of wisdom and perspective that every late middle-ager deserves to enjoy, in spite of the emerging deficit of future years. But, sooner or later, age seems to catch up on us and, very often, after a health crisis for instance, the scars of our actual chronological score make themselves apparent. It is then that we realise that this same body that has served us well up to now and has taken all the punishment we've thrown at it can start to let us down.

In relation to how we handle this, there is the risk that we may frantically attempt to delay the inevitable cosmetic, bodily signs of ageing and push against this rising tide with blithe denial, only to miss out on the many opportunities to redefine ourselves positively in later life and successfully manage the more important psychological adjustments we may need to make. For, when we cast a cold eye over all the things that we associate with ageing, it is sometimes difficult to escape the negative – whether that is fear of loss of freedom or a loss of vitality or even fear of downright boredom.

When you were young the future seemed full of infinite possibility and you were blind to all things finite and mortal. As you became middle aged, responsibilities grew but so, probably, did the respect you received for your expertise, status and accomplishments, as well as the sense of natural authority that seems to accompany middle age. Let's face it – if you couldn't solve the problem, it may simply have been insoluble. But let's also be honest – perhaps a little arrogance crept into this sense of mid-life authority; the young and the old may *both* have felt bullied by you!

Yet what a difference a decade or two can make, in terms of the status that human beings attract as they age – a standing which seems to peak in midlife and then trough. Although ageing is certainly a gift and truly a once-in-a-lifetime opportunity, as we age we come under pressure to make sure every remaining day counts and that we can live the life we want, all life long.

Perhaps you are also starting to introspect a little. You may begin, for example, to take stock of things that are slowly changing, such as sense of power and authority, which you may feel is slowly leaking away. You may, in compensation, begin to look back on a lifetime of days lived well (which, it is to be hoped, cancel out those that weren't), and you may try and distil these experiences into insights from which others may benefit. This is the gift that older people often endeavour to share with people in their midst, so that the younger generation will learn, at an earlier stage, the lessons you have learned in your longer life. But, so often, younger members of society are not willing to listen to those of sage years and see your advice as detrimental to their generational birthright to experience the present and the future fully, with all its ups and downs. The true meaning of independence for your offspring may be royally to repeat the same blunders that you made in your own life.

Active independent lives are the reality for many older people and you may still be very active in contributing to community and public life at local and/or national level, but what if those contributions aren't fully recognised, acknowledged or appreciated, and older people are not seen as the assets that they truly are? This harsh reality may especially apply when older people informally take on the care of a physically ill spouse or an adult child with learning difficulties. Or take the particularly common case of minding the grandchildren – a gesture which can save the parents the cost of a small mortgage in monthly childcare fees. If this is you, do you feel acknowledged and appreciated? Or do you feel taken for granted? Do you enjoy the opportunity this role brings to meet new people at the school gates, as you collect children from school, come hail, rain or shine? Or do you feel resentful about the time you have to give to this role, when you could be pursuing your own interests?

Stereotyping hurts

Perhaps, through picking up this book, you are thinking fully for the first time about all the different factors that can be associated with ageing and the boxes that older people can too readily be put into. Stereotyping of, and discrimination against, older people has received only a fraction of the attention that is devoted to understanding other forms of discrimination, such as racism or sexism. Stereotypes, by their very nature, never tell the full story. The classic stereotype of later life is often quite pathological, namely one of an ageing body, in contrast to the idealised fit and lean body of our youth. Whereas a youthful body is associated with beauty, energy, grace and optimism, an ageing body can evoke images of ugliness, feelings of pity, repulsion, disgust and, in its extreme images, even a sense of moral degeneration and failure.

There seems little doubt that the roots of stereotyping and discrimination against older people partly lie in our obsession as a society with youth and beauty and how it can be maintained at all costs (which many older people themselves will buy into). Other ageist stereotypes are equally negative (for instance that all older people are senile or cognitively impaired or are a burden on society) and all are ultimately damaging, as these misconceptions may be taken on board by the individuals themselves and can add to their fear and isolation. They also can build barriers between young and old – especially if older people are portrayed as a drain on resources.

Such stereotypes rather conveniently ignore the last time you had to bail out your offspring financially or abandon your own plans to look after sick grandchildren. Ageism (or negative treatment of people on the basis of their age) is undoubtedly fuelled by the creation of such stereotypes. Ageist behaviours that you or those you know may have encountered include being talked down to, having people accord less weight to your opinions, needs and beliefs, and taking your concerns such as your health and welfare less seriously.

Ageist attitudes may also include viewing a lower standard of living as acceptable for older people or seeing paid employment as the only work of value, believing thus that retirees are not productive or have nothing to contribute to society. Indeed, ageism could be described as an offence against equal opportunity, in that age can be a greater barrier than ethnicity or gender to full social and economic participation in the community.

Society seems deeply ageist, therefore, and I suggest that this is all based on fear – we fear advancing years, losing our physical and mental abilities and attractive physical appearance as well as our power, status and independence. As a defence against this anxiety, we seek to distance ourselves from older people, which is how we fear the future might look for ourselves when we are older. Indeed, ageist humour, such as that featured on birthday cards for anyone over 40, allows us to deny the reality of our own ageing. After all, it is all just a joke. Thus we seek to avoid reflecting on our own mortality, which, far from being a morbid exercise, can actually help all of us to prioritise issues in our life and move on from the past.

The form of discrimination that is ageism is, arguably, more prevalent today than in the past. In modern societies where other forms of discrimination such as racism or sexism have been challenged, it can be disconcerting to encounter such devaluative attitudes for the first time, simply because we are old.

For instance, something as seemingly simple as moving house can throw everything into disarray when an older person falls ill. The following (based on a variety of similar cases I have encountered in clinical practice) makes the point:

> I am 69 years of age and four years ago I retired from a job as a senior civil servant. I live alone, having been divorced from my wife of forty years just before my retirement. I was diagnosed with bipolar disorder in my late thirties but the disorder was well controlled through medication. However, I was advised to reduce my lithium dose over the years because of a

deterioration in kidney functioning. I made a decision to move to the country and came off the remaining low dose of medication shortly afterwards, as I was fed up with blood tests and felt I that changing my lifestyle had eliminated a lot of my stress, much of which was caused by my working life.

Unfortunately I began to become unwell again, experiencing anger outbursts, racing thoughts and severe insomnia. I contacted my previous psychiatrist who had known me well but he said he couldn't see me, as I no longer lived within his catchment area. He said he would write to my new GP with details of my medication and blood tests and said he would request that I should be referred to a local community mental health team for monitoring and support during my relapse. Unfortunately the letter took nearly ten days to arrive, during which time I was almost admitted to hospital.

Because of my age, the GP promptly got in touch with the local older persons community mental health team, believing they were the most appropriate service to meet my needs. I then received a phone call from a community psychiatric nurse, who said the referral was being passed to the local general adult psychiatry team, because I had a pre-existing condition and was not 'a new case' of mental illness and therefore didn't qualify for the old age service. Although I was relieved not to be labelled as geriatric and eventually got help from the adult community team, for nearly a month I had experienced a very severe crisis, which could have been eased had I not been the victim of miscommunication and bureaucracy.

I had lost the excellent support I had had for many years from my previous doctor, but had expected that this could be simply reinstated when I moved to a different catchment area. I really think there should be clarity as to which team a patient should be entitled to see – the GP didn't seem to know, which I found strange. This whole experience has clouded my move to my new home and has left me feeling very vulnerable.

Clearly service and organisational issues, which have nothing to do with addressing patient priorities, can become serious obstacles that impact directly on older people and lead to unnecessary suffering and distress.

Collusion

Equally, we are not purely the victims in these situations, as many of us may have colluded for years in disclaiming our rightful age in a myriad of ways, often expressing astonishment when finally confronted with reality. We may feel in a sense doubly surprised by the reactions of others to our ageing bodies, changes to which, perhaps, have been denied and disavowed from within for so long – and caricatured from without – by a society that still seems threatened by silver hair and wrinkles. How often do the media present images, airbrushed surely, of age-defying beauties in their seventies or even eighties, which older people are invited to be impressed by – and to emulate?

Even when the proverbial writing has been inscribed on the wall and our chronological score is unmistakable, the unacceptable truth of age can be buried in ever deeper layers of denial, as we ourselves stigmatise our *own* age cohort and label our peers as being out of touch, useless, in bad shape or unattractive and boring. It is testament to the power of labelling and stereotyping that people who are apparently defenceless targets of these forces may themselves hold onto similar hackneyed ideas of others of the same age or generation – or even of a younger generation. I know of one feisty lady, still dyeing her hair and wearing full makeup in her late eighties, who berated her 60-something daughter for letting her hair go grey, thus ruining, for observers, the mother's painstakingly maintained fiction of youth.

I have often noticed that older people who defy the more negative stereotypes of ageing in other ways are presented in the popular media as bizarre or comical. Positive stereotypes may create an 'idealised' older person, who proves that age is 'all in the mind' by a triumph of will over physiology; stories of older people being outrageous by doing a parachute jump at 85 or even robbing a bank are beloved by the popular media. Other examples of positive stereotypes could include the 'golden ager', such as the perfect grandparent who embodies traits of wisdom, trust and kindness, or the 'silver surfer', who is active, independent and up to date or 'with it', especially about technology. There was more than a grain of truth to this last image, as older people were avid users of the early internet in 1990s America – so that they could surf the stock market whilst attending their active retirement groups!

The problem with all the positive stereotypes, though, is that they are no less fickle or unrealistic than their negative counterparts. Indeed, they can rapidly flip over into negative ones – if the illusion of perfection is shattered by illness, for example.

If every generation needs its role models, and they do, with older people no being exception, those who can set realistic examples for seniors may be people who have appreciated their core talents and developed and achieved mastery in them. The example of Nelson Mandela comes to mind as an older person whose political skill was developed through many years of captivity and deprivation. The person that emerged from his incarceration was the epitome of dignity and statesmanship, someone whose example inspired respect and compromise and formed the basis of a non-violent transition to democracy in South Africa.

Such precedents require noting by a society permeated by media-driven, stereotyped portrayals of its oldest members, who ultimately are in danger of absorbing these negative attitudes themselves. This can have a highly detrimental impact on older people's expectations of and belief in what life has to offer them, adding to a sense of isolation and rejection.

For the reality is that, despite all these fears and efforts to fight ageing, *remarkably little changes as we grow older*. You are not evicted from your body, nor from your passions or interests, and most people still feel largely the same on the inside, even if the exterior all-weather paint is cracking a little. We should all in reality be enormously thankful for our bodies, which function remarkably well, despite years (particularly the early adult ones) of punishment, toxins and downright neglect. And not every depiction of older people is entirely negative; there are many softer images portraying later years in quite tranquil, peaceful, even desirable terms to be found in our popular media. Maybe, when the pace of life is too swift and expectations too high, it can be comforting for exhausted youth to observe with relief the repose that the opposite pole of the human lifespan can bring.

If we manage to resist ageism, however difficult that is, given its pervasive and sometimes quite obnoxious nature, we are free to develop and change and even grow, rather than endlessly trying to recover the irretrievable.

Lessons from other times ...?

Was there ever an historic golden era for older people that we can look back to, contrast with the present era and bemoan its passing? We may cling onto romanticised beliefs that multiple generations lived together under the same roof, with the young venerating the old and respect invariably moving against gravity, trickling upwards from younger folk to the old. This simplicity, however, would ignore the fact that gerontophobia (fear of old age) has existed for centuries, if not millennia. Aristotle was known to have called older people small-minded, malicious and ungenerous. There is evidence, moreover, that hunter-gatherer societies such as the Inuit tribes in Alaska, among others elsewhere, killed their older members when they became a burden on the rest of the community or were unable to hunt. In most traditional societies, you were generally given respect only as long as you were still useful. Grandmothers tended to fare better than grandfathers, as a rule, as their childminding role was deemed useful, whereas older men who lost the energy to hunt and catch prey could end up becoming the prey themselves.

On occasion, if older people were deemed to be the repository of healing or of ancient wisdom or knowledge essential to survival (such as the waterhole location), they retained high status within tribes or communities. Adjudicating disputes between younger tribe members was also a role for tribal elders; however, in general, it was only if older people held onto resources such as land that they also held onto their exalted position; prematurely distributing your assets to the younger generation came with not only a health but also a stature warning. Of course, in pre-industrial societies, there were proportionally fewer older people, due to high mortality rates, so those that did survive or exist had a scarcity value and retained a certain privilege – but only until they became a burden on others. And the notion that, in pre-industrial times in Western Europe, extended families lived under the same roof is also somewhat mythical – nuclear families living in one dwelling seem to have been the norm for as long as census records have been available.

Whatever standing they may have had previously, there seems little doubt that modernisation, with the arrival of the industrial revolution, steadily eroded the status of older people. New skills in urban centres were felt to be of greater value than working pastorally on the land, and the mystique of old age gradually evaporated. It was somewhat ironic that, as the health and social positions of older people improved with better medical care and other benefits, the social importance of older people declined steadily during the late nineteenth and twentieth centuries. It is also strange to reflect that, as the need for physical strength and energy has diminished with mechanisation and technology, many older people still find barriers to their participation in society and the wider economy.

... and from other places?

If it is true to say we shouldn't become attached to romanticised notions of how older people were perceived in pre-literate and pre-industrial societies (as, basically, you either contributed and were useful or you could be discarded), what is the present position of older people in other principally non-European cultures around the world? Those not from such a culture might look on wistfully and enviously at friends and neighbours from non-Western or ethnic backgrounds who, on the surface, appear to have multiple, intergenerational and extended family linkages buffering them from some of the effects of isolation and enforced changes that occur as we age. Some of us might imagine that older people have a more privileged position in certain societies, picturing respected grandparents in Italy, or in other Mediterranean countries, as important members of one big happy family, sharing in the bounty of the thoroughly integrated family dinner table. It is as if children are brought up to know that they will eventually exchange roles with their parents and will dutifully step in to look after them.

It is a simplification, however, to suggest that older people automatically have a happier lot just because they live outside the Western bloc of nations. China, despite its Confucian tradition of filial piety and respect for elders, recently introduced a law stipulating a minimum level of support parents can expect from their adult children, even allowing seniors to take their children to court for neglect. China also has to cope with the fallout of its 'one child' policy, which means quite simply that there are fewer numbers of carers to look after its senior citizenry. Some societies that have become more 'Westernised', such as Japan, have seen a fall off in the level of respect and automatic reverence shown to older people and a corresponding rise in the demand for adequate state reimbursement and availability of services and benefits for seniors. It may be surprising for some to learn that retirement homes are no longer a social taboo across Asia, as the numbers of older people increase and as families disperse, due to changing lifestyles, industrial development and migration.

However, many Indians still live in joint family units, with the eldest continuing to act as head of the household. The role older people serve in India can include minding grandchildren, dispensing advice on financial investments and retaining asset ownership, ironing out the details of traditional wedding rituals and issuing decrees to resolve intra-family conflicts. Much of the Korean regard for ageing is also rooted in Confucian values that dictate that one must respect one's parents and emphasise the duty of care for ageing members of the family. Even outside the family unit, Koreans are socialised to respect and show deference to older individuals, as well as authority figures in general. It also seems to be the case that, among Asian and other ethnic minority communities living in the West, close contact with extended family members, including elders, is more common, along with co-residence under the same roof, at least for a generation or two after arrival in the host country.

In essence, there is little doubt that cultural perspectives can have an enormous effect on our experience of growing older and that, in Western society, older people are removed with indecent haste from the community and relegated to hospitals and nursing homes as if ageing were an inherently shameful experience. Ironically, despite today's technologically advanced era, which could promote and directly assist independent living for many older people, and despite living longer and more healthily, older people in many Western societies seem more frequently to 'end up' in nursing home care than is the case in other parts of the world. If ageing tends to be seen by certain societies as an undesirable state, reducing physical beauty, functioning and bringing one closer to death, what better way to bolster this denial than by rendering old age an illness or pathology, needing custodial care (allowing the 'victims' to become invisible to the rest of us).

If the roots of ageism, especially in Western society, are a fear of the cosmetic aspects of ageing and the tying of an individual's value to their productivity, which inevitably wanes, I feel the saddest aspect is the belief and fear instilled in all of us that we are destined to become an ever greater insult to the collective eyes of society. Very many start out adult life by raucously celebrating non-conformity, yet seem destined to end life deeply ashamed of not conforming to a youthful ideal. Have you ever been afraid of being a burden on the younger generation or felt that a hurried and terse phone call you received from a busy son or daughter was made out of obligation, rather than genuine love or concern? Despite this, we always make allowances for them and their hectic lives.

Nobody ever suggests the younger generation are a burden on society, in spite of what the latest crime statistics tell us. Yet we often willingly move 'out of the way' to retirement communities, assisted living facilities or nursing homes. It takes a lot of guts and sheer bloody mindedness to reject the admonition, 'you can't do that', which is regularly flung at older people. 'You can't do that' applies to a whole range of activities, including having an opinion even on matters that impinge on your own well-being. Perhaps the most toxic, insidious aspect of ageism is the way subconscious attitudes exist to deny older people their fair share of resources and to discriminate against an entire section of society.

The same wider society may assume its eldest members are too frail to live independently, or to drive safely or to travel abroad or even sell property, and the same society frequently insists on stepping in and restricting the freedom of older people to prevent such 'inappropriate' activity. Older people may, however, become rapidly deskilled if not allowed to exist independently and to choose when they may need help. We may say such 'protective' actions are taken with the best of intentions, but it may be at the expense of the morale and spirit of an entire generation.

Perspectives on wealth
It is said that the biggest determinants of quality of life are health and wealth, although in my view no amount of

personal wealth can compensate for loss of, or compromise in, one's state of health and physical well-being. Wealth in the material sense is more than just a set of figures in a bank account, however, and should refer to the quality of our environment, both physical and social, and the range of informal and formal supports available to us, should we require them. I shall have a lot more to say about this.

The safety net of social and healthcare support and services that older people increasingly depend on has been underpinned by an unwritten contract between the generations for decades, ever since the introduction of a modern welfare state. These assumptions are increasingly being challenged, however, as people of working age are told to prepare to receive the basic state pension at a later age than ever before. Meanwhile, they may be struggling to afford their own homes, attain permanent jobs whilst juggling childcare responsibilities and trying to manage high personal debt. It may be galling for them to see older people 'swanning about' with good pensions, using up scarce healthcare resources, availing of free prescriptions and qualifying for a whole range of benefits such as free travel and other discounts, while they themselves strain to make ends meet. (This could represent fodder for strong animosity between the generations, if not a social revolution, were it not for the fact that large tracts of resources are, in fact, channelled towards the young, in terms of free education or childcare in particular, in most economies.)

While some people pursue money to attain financial security in retirement (and it can also take on a symbolic value that colours our self-image), the building of a nest egg is largely dependent on educational attainment and occupation, and real income for most will fall in retirement. Income inequality in many industrialised nations (particularly in the UK and the US) can grow significantly, as state pensions may offer only a third of one's pre-retirement income. Older people may find their self-esteem further eroded by such loss of earning potential if they still struggle with residual mortgages, debts, the ongoing support of adult dependents who are un- or under-employed, or the maintenance of second families.

Politicians have stealthily rolled back on many of the hard-earned entitlements gained during the nineteenth and twentieth centuries, which offered a modicum of dignity and comfort to people after a lifetime of hard work. Clichés used in the media, such as 'silver tsunami' and 'ticking demographic time bomb', appear to justify the unpicking of a range of state welfare benefits that risks producing real pensioner poverty for many who depended on them.

Older people all too frequently have to liquidate their assets to pay for the cost of continuing care for themselves or for a spouse or partner in a nursing or residential home. Only the very wealthy, it seems, can cushion themselves against the cost of exorbitant, and frequently sub-standard, long-term institutional care – for everyone else, the very roof over their head is at risk. The cost of medical care and personal home care may also be impossible to predict, or to insure against, as people live longer with chronic illness. Of course, as time goes on, increasing levels of physical and mental frailty at the extremes of age are likely to create growing dependence on professional assistance for activities of simple daily living.

While younger people rarely envy the state of health of older people, they may resent the concentration of assets among the older generation (in the United States, for instance, according to Deloitte University Press, up to 70 per cent of household wealth is owned by people over 60).[3]

---

3   Val Srinivas and Urval Goradia, *The Future of Wealth in the United States: Mapping Trends in Generational Wealth*, New York: Deloitte University Press, 2015, p. 13.

Indeed, more fortunate senior citizens *are* quite financially independent, through a lifetime's accumulated assets, and can avoid economic hardship. However, far from being a burden on society, they very often actively transfer resources to the younger generations during their lifetimes. Their support of the younger, 'high expectation' generation has kept many a young family afloat, even if such transfer of support has been hidden, or dressed up as a living legacy to which the young people feel entitled.

The greater future reliance on private pension provision for income replacement after retirement is somewhat untested for future generations. Ensuring adequate resources is now more than ever the responsibility of each individual and the implication is that low-income earners will face considerable disadvantage in their retirement. The absolute reality is that inadequate income level in retirement is going to have a major impact on anxiety, stress and depression rates; and severe loss of income is likely to impact on people's ability to participate in their community at many levels. A basic level of income relative to pre-retirement earnings thus may be crucial to a good experience of old age. Yet it is wise to keep in mind Gandhi's exhortations to keep an overall perspective on money, as expressed in the words often attributed to him: 'It is health that is real wealth and not pieces of gold and silver.'

Gandhi may also have been referring to the riches potentially to be derived from our social and physical environment, which are assets that may be intangible in terms of numerical calculation but which crucially form the biggest backdrop to our well-being and thriving. If older people live in neighbourhoods where crime is rampant, where senior citizens are invisible, isolated and excluded, their well-being is likely to suffer additionally, in repeating cycles of social division and deprivation. By contrast, where older people are included, where they have access to security, good-quality physical infrastructure and the natural environment, they, like every member of society, will be wealthy in the broadest sense of the word.

From the biological to the existential

Many older people, despite facing a shortage of years ahead, have a surplus of time in which to reflect and ruminate on some of the more existential life issues that tend to surface as the pace of life and activity slows down. Some may face a sense of despair when they think about mortality and unresolved life issues. Some may be anxious about dying or losing their independence incrementally or they may worry excessively about past mistakes, regrets and missed opportunities from their early lives, an activity which, sadly, tends to edge out any further dreams or ambitions. Maybe our inner disciplinarian inflicts the psychological equivalent of grievous bodily harm on us for failing to achieve adequate levels of fame, infamy or fortune. This regret circuit often takes place alongside the aforementioned profound denial of ageing and lack of identification with older people.

Existential themes and challenges that may burden older people in their ponderings may not just relate to the past but may also reflect a sense of frustration about the transitory character of life, as we grapple with the ultimate religious and spiritual questions. As for the future, people may become paralysed by procrastination or an inability to cope, as our world seems to shrink. A safety-first mindset may take over and older people may withdraw from new challenges or unfamiliar experiences, seeing threats to physical or emotional security where, frankly, none exists.

If, as I have pointed out, our self-image is entirely wrapped up in youthful physique or external appearance, then most people are in for a rude awakening. The shock of realising one's chronological age can be quite acute and invariably arrives when someone else, frequently a stranger, responds to us automatically and quite unconsciously in a particular way that denotes our changed and senior status. One acquaintance of mine, still active and productive well into her eighties, said it happened for her when the driver of a taxi she was getting out of was approached by another potential fare and said, 'Just let me help this old lady get down first'. The courtesy of being offered a pensioner's discount at the till can be blissful for one's budget but blistering for the ego. It can be even more startling when a senior discount is applied without even an inquiry as to one's eligibility. Still, in spite of the fact that mirrors rarely lie, there may be the compensation that, in very advanced age, diminishing eyesight seems to camouflage the wrinkles.

Although the prospect of reversing mortality has always had universal appeal, the reality is that running repairs to the human body can only temporarily stem the tide of ageing and no currently marketed intervention has yet been proven to slow, stop or reverse it. Quite simply, the idea of a fountain of youth is a mirage and the oasis that we should search for instead is an acceptance of our finite score, with a quiet determination to squeeze every last drop out of life. It has been said that worrying about death, whether ours or that of someone we love, is as futile as worrying about who will attend our funeral, yet it is a universal fear. Some people may also worry incessantly about what death will actually be like when our 'turn' comes – will we die in our sleep as we may desperately hope or will the world as we experience it end in some big medical crisis or drama?

However, as we age, the fear of dying may become just the tip of our slowly melting iceberg of life, which gradually reveals fears about isolation or loneliness, loss of dignity and independence, and pain and suffering during the process of dying, to name but a few elements of this monolithic anxiety that may intrude into human consciousness.

Society's reaction to death has changed quite fundamentally in recent decades, in that we seem to experience a more intense discomfort around it compared to other generations, who had to contend with high infant mortality rates and elevated pre-antibiotic mortality as a result of infectious diseases, such as pneumonia. The rituals of public grief and mourning appear to have dissipated in recent years, even to the extent that we prefer to use words such as 'lost' or 'passed away' or 'passed', as opposed to dying, such is our unease about living amidst death. The end result of this collective denial is that death and dying goes underground; it becomes medicalised and is almost perceived as a personal failing rather than as a very natural event. It is astonishing to reflect on the fact that, since 1951, in the UK and the US, it has been illegal to list 'old age' on its own as a cause of death on death certificates.

The skill of admitting the existence and inevitability of death is, therefore, far from a morbid exercise. We can, instead, decide to reclaim all the energy that goes into denying and repressing death, and staving off the signs of one's encroaching mortality in all its forms, by embracing life and all its associated opportunities more fully. While this is admittedly a lot easier to declare and aspire to than to accomplish or master, nonetheless successfully taking ownership of this challenging mindset can help people of *all* ages to view old age not as synonymous with death but with living.

It was the twentieth-century psychologist Erik Erikson who argued that the fear of ageing keeps us from living fully, writing: 'Lacking a culturally viable ideal of old age, our civilisation does not really harbour a concept of the whole life.'[4] This is what we can start to change and this is what I want to address in the rest of this book.

---

4   Erik H. Erikson and Joan M. Erikson, *The Life Cycle Completed*, New York: Norton, 1997.

PART II

Maintaining well-being: challenges and opportunities

So much that we learn about the landscape of later life encourages us to think about it as very different from earlier life stages, with very different requirements. But, as I have said, older age seems to span a number of different ages within itself. So I would like to suggest the opposite: that older age is part of a continuum in which our most important needs (and abilities) don't change at all.

The givens of human nature

Universal laws dictate that, in order to survive, every single living thing must continually maintain and rebuild itself by drawing the nutrition it needs from the environment. As human beings, we all have a distinct set of physical and emotional needs, and innate resources to help us attain them, which together have been termed our 'human givens'. They provide a meaningful snapshot of what it is to be human, and what consciously and unconsciously drives many aspects of our behaviour. While it goes without saying that we have basic physical needs – such as food, shelter, sleep and air to breathe – that must be fulfilled in order to survive, decades of health and social psychology research have shown that the meeting of emotional needs is just as important. When we meet our emotional needs appropriately through balanced use of our resources, psychological distress and much mental ill health will be entirely absent or significantly ameliorated.

Our ability to thrive largely depends on emotional and psychological well-being, not just at the level of the individual but also at the level of entire communities and societies.

The Human Givens framework identifies the range of emotional requirements for healthy existence, which are also the core drivers of our behaviour. When any of these key emotional needs is seriously unmet, there is threat to our physical and psychological well-being. It is also vitally important that these needs are met in a balanced fashion to ensure that we remain flexible and able to adapt when changes and challenges inevitably come our way. I like the definition that clinical psychologist and author Dr William F. Harley gives for an emotional need in his book *His Needs, Her Needs*, which looks at marriage and relationships. An emotional need, he says, is 'a craving that when satisfied leaves you with a feeling of happiness and contentment, and, when unsatisfied, leaves you with a feeling of unhappiness and frustration.'[1]

However, we don't have just a single emotional need; there are a number of emotional prerequisites for health – just as we can't rely on only one source of food to keep us healthy but instead create a balanced diet from a broad range of nourishment available to us.

---

1   Willard F. Harley, Jr, *His Needs, Her Needs: Building an Affair-Proof Marriage*, Oxford: Lion Hudson Publishers, 2011.

Let's take a look at the emotional needs that have been identified and which need fulfilment throughout our lives.

Security

Our need for security is fundamental. We need a safe territory and environment if we are to live without undue fear, develop fully and have space to grow. This manifests from our earliest moments – very young children feel safe to venture forward and explore only when they know that loving parents or caregivers 'have their backs'. As life goes on, we will feel insecure if we don't feel we fit in (perhaps we are shy at school or look different or have a different sexuality); if we don't feel safe where we live (because the area is unsafe or because the people we rely on are cruel or don't have our best interests at heart); if we don't have sufficient income to get by; if our jobs are under threat; or if we are unkindly treated by those who have a significant role in our lives. Older people who find themselves trapped in unsuitable environments with high levels of crime or antisocial behaviour or in unscrupulously run care homes, will feel especially vulnerable; and such a lack of physical security is likely to be extremely detrimental to well-being.

Autonomy

Having a sense of volition or control over our own lives is crucial. Who doesn't remember the first freedom to make decisions and choices in life as empowering? We need to feel that our input counts, and to be able to pursue our own goals and follow our dreams. Unfortunately, sense of control can be all too readily compromised in later years, if older people are forced to relinquish control over their assets, their homes or are deemed incapable of making even simple decisions. Loss of control in selecting a course of action in life, however small, is likely to lead to frustration, dependency and an anxious aversion to change.

Attention

An exchange of attention – giving and receiving it in relatively equal measure – is essential for the development of emotional, cognitive and social skills. This attention exchange begins at the very start of life, when all is well, with mother and baby looking lovingly into each other's eyes as the baby feeds. We can see children blossom when they are given positive attention for their efforts or ideas. Attention is so important that, for children deprived of sufficient positive attention (perhaps because parents are too busy with their work lives or their phones), negative attention garnered through bad behaviour may be better than none. Paying attention to each other forms part of our group bond as a gregarious species, and helps us maintain a shared model of reality. Some people struggle with giving attention, such as those on the autistic spectrum, and this contributes to their difficulties in fitting into social situations, which in turn impacts negatively on their well-being.

Older people can struggle to get their attention needs met, due to their being marginalised by a society that prefers to deny any signs of physical decay and human frailty. Their concerns may be dismissed and, both individually and as a group, they are often excluded and ignored. The 'corralling' of older people together in nursing homes or institutions is an example of such exclusion. All this may result in what is often dismissively termed 'attention-seeking behaviour'. While such behaviour among younger people may be portrayed as a rite of passage or a cry for help, when it manifests in older people it may instead be portrayed as selfishness, whingeing and envy of eternal youth.

Intimacy

Emotional connection with others in the form of friendships and loving relationships is one of the greatest joys of human existence. We all need at least one person in this world who accepts us for who we are – flaws and all; a person who will offer us unconditional support and be biased in our favour, to the point of defending and supporting us through thick and thin. A range of people may offer us such love and support throughout our lives – parents or parent figures initially, then friends, spouses, workmates and colleagues.

However, older people, of course, are likely to experience gradual loss, through illness and death, of the people who were their emotional confidants, friends and supporters.

Such a high level of loss would be devastating and difficult for any other generation (in peacetime) to imagine, yet most older people resignedly weather these storms without complaint.

Older people may also be denied physical touch and intimacy – not every older person has loving grandchildren patiently forming a queue for cuddles, and there are still many sanctions and barriers around the expression of sexuality in older people, which continues to be treated as a taboo subject.

Community

The need to be part of something larger than ourselves and be connected to a wider network beyond family through work, leisure pursuits and community activities stems from our evolutionary past as hunter-gatherers in a pre-historic era. Group membership offered humans relative safety from a range of hazards, including other predators, and allowed people to pool resources and form collaborative teams, in order to fight off threats or build communities and the structures to support them. Being an outcast from the tribe meant mortal danger – a persistently ingrained fear of being ostracised still resonates amongst most of us, as we carve out our identities in terms of membership of one group or tribe or another.

For older people who are less mobile or who experience illness, community participation in the real world may be severely compromised, impacting negatively on their ability to meet this important emotional need. Virtual communities, joined through social media, have become ever more popular in recent years, but an older non-tech-savvy generation may get left behind. Conversely, social media may form a lifeline for many older people who take it on themselves to acquire new skills and abilities to use devices such as phones, tablets and laptops, enabling them to stay in almost constant touch with family and even make new friends.

Status

Knowing that we have a valued place in each of the groupings to which we belong is another important need. The respect afforded us for our role is central to our sense of self and overall identity. Such roles can be wide-ranging and can include being a caring parent, being respected at work, being appreciated for specific creative or sporting skills, having status for a quality such as being reliable, being caring, being able to make people laugh, and so on. Status also reinforces our sense of social acceptance and reassurance that we will not be expelled from the tribe.

Older people who are active and energetic may have little difficulty fulfilling this need through new activities after retirement from the workplace, whereas others whose whole identity was centred on their work or who may no longer be fit and active may struggle significantly.

Competence and achievement

An awareness of our own competence, abilities and skills, without which we may feel inadequate, is a crucial building block of self-esteem. We absolutely need to feel good about ourselves. This can be further enhanced if we have the opportunity to exercise these skills by contributing to our communities. The self-confidence that comes from having knowledge and skills increases our ability for resilience, which is vital when we are faced with unexpected challenges.

Older people, despite previously being recognised as highly knowledgeable and experienced, may struggle to convince others that their competencies are still intact or, indeed, up to date. Or they may simply fall victim to the stereotype that, if they are doddery and old, they can't be good for much.

Privacy

For all of us, in the rapidly moving world that we live in, attention gets divided and information overload can engulf our memory and powers of concentration. We can easily find ourselves mechanistically and mindlessly moving from one novelty or experience to another unless we carve out private space from within hectic schedules. Having time to reflect upon, absorb and learn from our everyday experiences is essential as a means to regain energy and sense of perspective. For some people, regular walks in nature are their favoured way to 'regroup' and take stock. Others may have to snatch moments such as luxuriating in a bath or taking time to tune out while travelling from A to B.

But too much time in privacy can be counterproductive. Older people who spend a lot of time alone have excessive time to reflect and ruminate, resulting in negative thinking. Conversely, those living in communal settings such as nursing homes or other institutions may suffer a grave lack of privacy, having to experience intimate personal care as well as eat, sleep and entertain in public.

Meaning and purpose

We all need something to get up for in the morning, and that entails having a sense of meaning. Being purposefully mentally and physically stretched, without being stressed, can help buffer the harsh realisation of our own mortality. It may come from being helpful to others, contributing to our community or being aligned to causes or beliefs greater than ourselves and our own material needs. This higher-order emotional need essentially defines the essence of our humanity – the care and contribution that only we can make. As we grow older, the focus of our minds shifts towards integrating all our life experiences in a way that accords with our core ethical frameworks and beliefs. By reflecting on those principles and beliefs that we deem sacred, we are drawn to recognise not what is missing in our lives but what we have stood for all along and what has added value as we continually redefine our sense of purpose whilst we go on growing in years. For many older people, a meaningful life involves serving others and leaving a good legacy. Transcending self-interest along the journey of life requires a bigger worldview, and for many this allows the realisation that their lives were worthwhile and meaningful.

Deriving meaning from life is, therefore, one of the key tasks facing older people, and awareness and application of the Human Givens set of organising ideas can be a hugely helpful navigation aid. The attributes that allow us human beings to thrive in our environment are innate, universal, essential and accessible to everyone. They don't come from material achievement nor do they arise as a result of higher educational attainment. They may seem self-evident, yet they are quite profound.

Leaving these core principles and dimensions of human existence at the margins of our concerns, very often leads to a sense of incompleteness or unfinished business. There can be a sense that something is missing in our lives, even if it is not consciously missed. A central task, after all, is to make sense of life, and our part in it, realising what becoming more fully human entails. This includes accepting vulnerabilities, strengths and limitations as well as working on ways to more fully meet our needs. Owning and making sense of our personal life story, with all its ups and downs, missed and grasped opportunities and potential for yet realising many goals is crucial if we are to buffer challenges to our self-worth and self-esteem in later years.

Creating and adopting new and holistic forms of meaning makes up the bedrock of successful ageing. This helps us transcend frailty as we come to realise that we still share most, if not all, of the emotional and psychological requirements that our younger counterparts similarly struggle to attain. Older people won't continue to thrive if they just live off memories of the life they have already lived; human beings of *all* ages need the power to dream, to enable us to do something that can change tomorrow. There is no evidence that we dream less or love less with the passing of years – we can still cherish what we have and, even if we scale back our immediate ambitions for ourselves, our wise counsel may motivate the next generation to realise our unfinished pilgrimage in making this earth a better place.

Not a zero-sum game

It is important to realise that our emotional needs are not hierarchical – they overlap and interconnect, and they should be met in balance so that we are mentally healthy. Any significant lack of fulfilment of any one of these needs over a period of time takes a toll on both physical and emotional well-being. Conversely, needs can be met in unhealthy ways, which again will take its toll on well-being. We need a certain amount of attention, for example, but people who crave not just recognition but constant admiration and regard may display traits consistent with the narcissistic personality, with the result that they will lack empathy towards others. This may be very off-putting for other people and ultimately works against the excessively self-absorbed person, alienating them from those around them and reducing their prospects for intimately connecting with others.

We all need security, yet we also need to take risks to make progress in many areas of life; being too risk averse can be counterproductive, as it may make us vulnerable and incompetent in the face of real or unexpected danger.

If we focus overly on our private space and jealously guard privacy at all costs we run the risk of becoming isolated and not connecting with the community around us. Being in control and having free will is beneficial, but those obsessed with being constantly in control (so called control freaks) and micromanaging everyone else can cause havoc with other people's needs within families, work situations and larger communities. Those that they dominate may end up lacking initiative, creativity and satisfaction in life, being effectively pawns of others, rather than agents of their own free will. This, not surprisingly, can make people passive, resentful and downright unhappy, unprepared for and, ironically, resistant to change. Fortunately, to help us find ways to meet our essential emotional needs in balance, nature has given us a wealth of inbuilt resources.

Our innate human resources

Our innate resources are developed over time. They prevent us from mindlessly repeating old habits and allow us to grow and mature, choosing adaptive over maladaptive responses to the various challenges we encounter. We not only thrive emotionally but also, in the process, develop stamina and perseverance. A Human Givens perspective identifies our key resources as:

- **Emotions and instincts**
  Our emotions (physical sensations that we interpret – helpfully or unhelpfully) and instincts drive us to meet our needs. They lead us to take action (hence the motion component of the word e-motion), often in response to an external threat. When faced with danger, our bodies get us ready to fight our corner or to flee. Equally, a feeling of loneliness may impel us to do something to make new friends or a feeling of insecurity may lead us to learn new skills. Our emotions, therefore, have a vital role in our drive to survive and thrive. Acting instinctively, 'trusting our gut', is akin to trusting the collection of all our subconscious experiences, and there is no evidence that the power of this diminishes with age. The learned experience from all our years of being alive is a cumulative resource, even if it is not immediately apparent to the conscious mind. Of course, if our learned experience has not been positive (for example, a sense of learned helplessness arising from ongoing abuse during childhood or an over-sensitivity to bodily sensations that has resulted in excess anxiety), our instinct to keep safe may be unhealthily honed, and danger perceived in all sort of unlikely places – the right kinds of therapy can help with this.

- **Empathy**
  The ability to build rapport, empathise and connect with other people is a crucial skill that human beings develop in order to interact with and care for each other, and share as a group. Progress for both individuals and communities requires cooperation, and high-level communication skills enhance the likelihood of success in all our endeavours. Compassion, kindness and, indeed, selflessness depend on our being able to understand another person's perspective, and this underpins the ethical and moral framework of providing support for those who are most vulnerable – which may include ourselves as we age.

- **Memory**
  The ability to learn and build on the experiences we have is crucial for adding to our innate knowledge. Forming new memories is, perhaps, akin to adding layer upon layer to our minds, just like the rings added onto the trunk of a tree. Not all memories fade as we age and, even if short-term recall may be slower, our crystallised knowledge (such as vocabulary) or implicit memory (such as knowing how to drive or use a knife and fork) may remain very much intact. Making good use of what we know is a form of wisdom, which is an attribute highly correlated with older age.

- **Imagination**
  A powerful imagination allows us to problem solve creatively by trying out in our minds ideas and potential solutions to life's various challenges. Our imaginative faculties generate reality (we can put into practice what we have explored and rehearsed mentally first), and distinguish us from other mammalian life forms.

Imagination explains the extraordinary progress human beings have made in the last two millennia, pervading all realms of our existence, from academia to science and the arts. Daydreaming is part of the human condition and our ability to dream remains undiminished, irrespective of our chronological age. But, as with all other resources, we can unwittingly use our imagination against ourselves, through worrying and conjuring up catastrophe.

- **Perception**
  We perceive and understand the world unconsciously, through a subtle metaphorical pattern-matching process, whereby we relate sensations and experiences to what we already know. This process starts in the womb, where foetuses are programmed with templates for which completion will be sought in the outside world – such as the instinct, after birth, to look for a nipple-like object to get sustenance (milk). It doesn't have to be a nipple; it can be the teat of a bottle. The 'pattern', or template, is what the baby recognises. As we go through life, we use these templates, innate or learned, to organise our understanding of experiences we have and to give them meaning – in other words, what we perceive and make of things depends on the associations we hold for them. These could be positive: trying hard brings rewards; or negative: no matter what I do, it never works. Understanding this process and learning to uncouple unhelpful pattern matches by changing expectations and experience is an important skill.

- **Reason**
  We use reason consciously to check out emotions, analyse, plan and adapt. It enables us to question, 'fine tune', make contingency plans and discriminations. Reason tempers

the impulsivity of our emotional response and allows us to think in an organised, clear way to achieve knowledge and understanding. As a cognitive ability, it allows us to verify information, apply logic and consciously adapt our behaviour to changing circumstances. Only with a certain level of maturity can dispassionate reason come to dominate and to guide better and more balanced decision-making.

- **Enhanced awareness**
  This refers to the part of us that can step back and be more objective about our thoughts, feelings and conditioning. When we overly attach to our thoughts, we believe essentially that we *are* the thoughts, often critical, that float across our minds. By becoming more aware of our habitual modes of thinking, feelings and behaviour, and recognising that they don't have to govern us, we are better able to direct our attention and make empowering, conscious choices, rather than knee-jerk reactions. We can become more aware of the thinker behind the thought.

- **Dreaming**
  Dreaming is the brain's way to discharge any unexpressed emotionally arousing worries and ruminations from the day before, so we can face each new day afresh. Dreaming also helps preserve the integrity of our instinctive templates, which direct our actions and responses. (For instance, if we are bullied but routinely keep our mouths shut and don't express our anger, the anger instinct is likely to get dulled altogether. But if we 'act out' the unexpressed anger response in a dream, it stays intact.)
  Sleep is a balance between dream and non-dream sleep; in the latter, the brain carries out vital repair work to keep our stress levels low and our immune system healthy.

The suppositions of human nature – a template for life

It is clear to me that, as we grow in years, not a single emotional need becomes less important, nor do our innate resources for obtaining them (even our memory) necessarily diminish with the passage of time. The reverse could be argued, in fact, especially as many of our higher-order brain abilities, such as reason, empathy skills and intuition, seem to appreciate in value year by year. It is as if nature is rewarding us for having made it to life's later stages by giving us a dividend on an investment we never realised we had made: greater wisdom, insight and ability to reflect.

While there is little doubt that it may be the fittest among us that will survive, to me it is clear that it is the *wisest* among our species who are likely to do well also, especially in a modern environment where shrewd thinking skills are as crucial as, if not more important than, sheer physical strength. A wiser head may be readily able to compensate for a dearth of one particular resource, for example certain aspects of fluid memory, by making more use of detailed longer-term memories, which become rich narratives and stories. Some elders living in a communal institution such as a nursing home may trade need for privacy or autonomy for greater security, which may take precedence when independent living is no longer possible. Similarly, some older people, especially retired men, may yearn for the higher status they once enjoyed as an employee but, rather than becoming preoccupied and frustrated by this, may compensate by deepening relationships within their families or communities.

I am now going to look at the main areas of challenge that older people face, and will consider them through the lens of the need to meet key emotional and psychological needs, to throw different light on how they can best be handled.

Work life and retirement

There used to be a fairly widely held view that retirement was an event which could trigger ill-health, both physical and psychological – there is an old saying among family doctors that certifying a man unfit for work on medical grounds predicted the signing of a death certificate within a year. Recent research refutes this, however, and shows that retirement in itself does not cause damage to the health or well-being of the individual. The particular circumstances *leading* to retirement are relevant, however, including whether it is being entered into voluntarily, whether there are associated health issues, and the personal financial status and sources of social support available from within one's family or community.

When it comes to retirement, society has not yet woken up to the demographic revolution that has seen more years added to life expectancy in the last century than all of the previous millennia of human history combined. It is clear that the corporate world continues to behave as if very little has changed. People are still retiring at an age when they are neither old nor necessarily psychologically prepared for retirement. Retirement as it is currently construed does not meet the needs of older people seeking an active third phase of their life, as opposed to just existing or passively living out a third age, and is largely based on an outdated nineteenth-century view of the industrial workplace. It may indeed be the case, for many, that leaving work is the signal that 'middle age' is over and that a retiree belongs to a different social category.

The original meaning of retirement means withdrawal to a place of safety or refuge. When the term is applied to this stage in older people's lives, however, it sends a message of sanctioning a level of disengagement from society, which is essentially detrimental to the well-being of senior citizens. It's obvious that disengaging from society is not only disadvantageous to older people but also to society itself, which fails to benefit from intergenerational communication and resilience.

Clearly, from a mental well-being perspective, our work lives can help us fulfil many needs – for status, attention, sense of competence and achievement, community and, for many, meaning and purpose. Some professions do offer, if not an indefinite tenure of employment, at least a decent extension to the usual fixed-term contract. The famous American cardiac surgeon Dr Michael DeBakey's career in medicine spanned almost seventy-five years, as he continued to practise in medicine until his death at the age of 99 in 2008.

Enlightened organisations may extend greater flexibility to employees to help them achieve a better life–work balance at the latter stage of their careers. Some may be offered part-time hours, to entice them to remain working after 65 and continue to give the organisation the great gift of their experience, skills and their invaluable awareness of corporate culture and ethos – what greater acknowledgement of status and achievement could there be than that?

For those who don't expect such opportunities, it might be worth thinking about the impact of a work appraisal in your early sixties, that could encourage you to play to your strengths within the company or that could carve out a mentoring role, to ensure that your experience and knowledge was passed on to younger colleagues within the organisation. It meets the need for craving change and flexibility in relation to work commitments without fully relinquishing core expertise and talent. Perhaps it might be something to raise with your own human resources department, as a possibility for the future.

Of course, many older workers do nowadays choose to stay in the workplace beyond 65 or may even be obliged to, as pensionable age for some recedes further into the future. Some people may not, in fact, be able to retire because of the need to boost income. The ability of societies to fund statutory pension benefits will undoubtedly become strained, even if governments continue to increase the minimum age of pension entitlement.

So, among those who do leave their established employment, many continue to work part time or 'un-retire' to launch a completely new career. Paul Tasner, in his TED talk 'How I Became an Entrepreneur at 66', vividly highlighted the value of a different career path for 'ex-retirees' who re-launched themselves as entrepreneurs.[2] He pointed out the 70 per cent success rate of entrepreneurs aged over 55, compared with the 28 per cent success rate of their younger counterparts aged under 30.

Those who do choose to retire, and who are fortunate enough to retire in good health and with sufficient wealth, can look forward to the so-called '30:30 era', when thirty years of leisure and cut-price cinema tickets follows thirty years of hard endeavour – but it wasn't always so. In the past, by the time most people retired they had become run down through manual work or worn out and exhausted from the effort of bringing large families into the world. Far from being able to enjoy a cosy domestic bliss after a long working life, our ancestors frequently fell under the scythe of the grim reaper at far too young an age. Average life expectancy at birth in Britain in 1900 was about forty-seven years for a man and fifty for a woman. That has been steadily increasing over

2   Paul Tasner, 'How I Became an Entrepreneur at 66', Ted.com, June 2017, https://www.ted.com/talks/paul_tasner_how_i_became_an_entrepreneur _at_66; accessed 15 April 2022.

the last two generations in the UK, with life expectancy now standing at 79.4 years for men and 83.1 years for women in 2017, according to the Office for National Statistics.[3] You could argue that this longevity dividend represents arguably the greatest human achievement of the twentieth century, although it varies significantly between countries. In nations such as Japan, Italy and Germany, well over 20 per cent of the population is in the over-65 age category, whilst developing nations such as Niger, Uganda and Mali currently have the lowest proportion of senior citizens. This is set to change in the future.

The new mentality of retirement

At the start of retirement we may relish all those riches of time, once there is no longer an alarm clock sounding on Monday mornings, signalling the starting gun for the weekly grind and rat race. It's clear that the novelty of endless daytime television, manicuring the garden or taking time over tasks such as meticulously stacking the dishwasher or doing DIY chores, may rapidly wear thin. Many of us simply don't have the skills to motivate ourselves or to plan leisure and pleasure amidst all that free and unstructured time. That may come as a surprise to many because, for the past forty years, leisure activities or hobbies probably suffered from chronological starvation, being endlessly compressed by demands of work and home life in terms of the attention possible to give them. It would seem, therefore, that there will be no problem filling time pleasantly. But that doesn't

---

3   Office for National Statistics, *National Life Tables – Life Expectancy in the UK: 2017 to 2019*, Newport: Office for National Statistics, 2020, https://www. ons.gov.uk/peoplepopulationandcommunity/birthsdeathsandmarriages/ lifeexpectancies/bulletins/nationallifetablesunitedkingdom/2017to2019; Accessed 15 April 2022.

take account of human nature and those all-important needs we require fulfilling.

Our biggest challenge, simply put, is how to manage a clutter-free schedule without feeling lazy or going crazy! The half-day pre-retirement course that your employer may have grudgingly paid for now seems hopelessly insufficient – it may have made you an expert on tax and social welfare benefits, but what about the range of skills needed to journey successfully through the post-work years? This is where we need to consider the fulfilment of our need for some degree of control. No one is making us stay in bed till 11 a.m. or noon or not get dressed properly, and it is up to us to consider whether this feels like freedom – or being out of control.

So what is important is that individuals get their needs met in later life through means other than gainful employment (and, for some, life outside of work may always have been more important in this respect). You will need to consider for yourself which of the needs are most important for you to find new ways of fulfilling. Perhaps connection is most important or feeling valued or feeling that you have competencies to pass on, or feeling that you are doing something that matters. Many activities will deliver on all of these.

Or maybe more privacy is to be welcomed, time to give to solitary creative activities that require dedication and blocks of concentration.

There are very many opportunities, now that the expertise of older people is increasingly being recognised. Older people with different skill sets may be welcomed into schools as mentors or to offer off-curriculum or after-school activities. Charities always need people to donate time and skills. One man I know who had retired after a highly successful career in business offered his services to a UK Citizens Advice Bureau and found himself developing a whole new skill area of his own, becoming the go-to person for debt management advice and advocacy in repossession court cases.

Retirement in twenty-first-century terms is not only defined by individual priorities, goals and values but also by achieving a carefully crafted balance between paid employment, meaningful activity such as volunteering and time for leisure, family and hobbies. Without being overly prescriptive, it is up to each of us to decide the relative proportion of time and energy to invest in each one, or preferably all, of these domains in order to live life to the full in later years.

What to watch out for

Retirement may for some be a threat, to others a loss but for most of us a waking dream full of opportunity, waiting for us after years of toil and effort as we discussed earlier. Health and wealth status can be the biggest predictors of how this eagerly awaited phase of life will evolve, but the theme of personal reinvention is one that will likely emerge more and more. In fact, preparation for retirement is one that begins even decades before the event, with even relatively young workers now planning and considering pension provision at an early stage of their careers. By mid career the process of retirement, one could argue, should be well underway, long before the actual event when you hand in those retirement papers in exchange for a (one hopes, large) lump sum.

But in many ways retirement from paid employment should come with a government health warning similar to those emblazoned on cigarette packets and beer bottles. What happens if a person's expectations are not met, having retired, or if the best-laid plans and hopes are dashed through illness or other personal misfortune? Assumptions about the value and benefit of all that spare time may be misplaced; or the rural idyll that we moved to, which was coveted weekend after weekend during our working lives, may turn out to be a rural prison, as we lose contact with familiar friends and neighbourhoods. Retirement should, therefore, come with copious plan B's, in case plan A backfires, as frequently it does. How prepared are you to absorb shocks to your private pension pot in an economic downturn and have you coping or contingency plans in case you or a significant other experiences a health upset?

Engaging in a personal stock-take and pre-planning is crucial for the fruitful spending of the most precious commodity of time that any of us may ever get. Consider all the basics beforehand, such as whether you are someone who can cope with and manage unstructured time or prefer routine and structure. Should you wish to enlist outside support, a professional counsellor or psychotherapist will be especially well placed to help your retirement planning move forward apace, based on their fundamental knowledge of innate human needs and the resources that are active and available to obtain them.

But we have to acknowledge that, while retirement can offer a continued outlet for well-honed expertise and talent, sadly, for some, there may be too much time to introspect, regret and ruminate about unfulfilled opportunities or mistakes, which are an inevitable part of the journey of life. Older men who were previously stereotypically workaholic, for example, may become aware of the joy of nurturing and emotionally connecting with their children during retirement, and regret that this has happened all too late, if adult children have long left the nest before these belated parental insights and realisations. Death anxiety, frustration and a sense of a foreshortened future, along with alienation from 'mainstream' society and other losses or enforced changes, can be quite the toxic cocktail, producing a paralysing fear of death or a major depression. People who find themselves in this unfortunate position would benefit from seeking brief, solution-focused help (such as is offered by appropriately qualified psychotherapists who regularly work with older clients) to help them shift perspective and get meaning back into their lives again.

Physical health

As far as physical health in later life is concerned, there are two needs that can be hugely compromised – status and control. This section will look at the ways that fulfilment of these needs may be denied or taken away from older people and how it may be possible to reassert them.

First, I would like to acknowledge that health education has done a great service in instilling older people with the expectation that they can and should be proactive about improving and looking after their health as they age (taking control), as opposed to passively assuming that nothing can be done to steady the ship once illness strikes. There is also evidence that older people are not only living longer but also more healthily, and periods of poor health which come before the end of life are thankfully being compressed. For professionals working in any area of older people's health, however, it can be more than a little dispiriting to keep hearing management of acute and chronic illness in older adults being perpetually framed in crisis terms. We frequently hear the words 'silver tsunami' and 'age wave' when discussing the growing older population. We are also continually being told by health planners that there is a critical shortage in professionals trained to administer care to the rising tide of older people, who are inevitably destined to become patients. It is as if health mandarins are deliberately trying to scare older people away from the health services that they have so poorly designed in the first place!

Much of the rationale for health services dedicated to the needs of older people is the fact that older people frequently present with atypical features of illness, often creating delays in diagnosis and treatment. There is an old cliché amongst physicians in geriatric medicine (the name for the specialty concerned with looking after older patients) that, in respect of the clinical features of physical and mental illness, the atypical is typical. Urinary tract infections can present with dizziness, confusion and falls, while a myocardial infarction or classic heart attack can present with breathlessness, vomiting and weakness instead of chest pain.

Approximately 80 per cent of Americans over the age of 65 have at least one chronic disease, and 50 per cent have two or more, according to the Center for Disease Control and Prevention.[4] Not all chronic conditions are 'active' and some may behave like a dormant volcano over which one could safely build one's home, whereas others can significantly affect everyday functioning as well as causing sensory and cognitive impairments.

Perhaps the most common intervention to be performed by doctors is to write a prescription – older people will have more conditions requiring medication. It is estimated (according to the *Oxford Handbook of Geriatric Medicine*) that two-thirds of over-65s are on medication, with care-home residents being prescribed on average seven to eight different medications.[5] Being dependent on a range of drugs for daily survival may seem a particularly bitter, albeit essential, pill to swallow but

---

4   National Center for Health Statistics, 'Percent of U.S. Adults 55 and Over with Chronic Conditions', https://www.cdc.gov/nchs/health_policy/adult_chronic_conditions.htm; accessed 15 April 2022.

5   Jalpa A. Doshi, Thomas Shaffer and Becky A. Briesacher, 'National Estimate of Medication Use in Nursing Homes: Findings from the 1997 Medicare Beneficiary Survey and the 1996 Medical Expenditure Survey', *Journal of the American Geriatrics Society*, Vol. 53, No. 3 (2005), pp. 438–43.

this polypharmacy (taking of multiple medications) has an even more toxic element because older patients frequently experience a greater burden of side effects and adverse reactions to individual medicines, as well as a much greater risk of adverse effects from all the drugs interacting on each other.

It has been estimated, according to one US study, that between 10 and 30 per cent of all hospital admissions among older patients in primary care are related to medication complications.[6] Metabolism of drugs in older people may be slower, and excretion of medicines and drug distribution may also vary. So it is very important that an older person is prescribed a reduced medication dosage to prevent such a dangerous accumulation of drugs and emergence of side effects. Older people often don't drink sufficient water (in contrast to younger people, who are rarely seen without a designer water bottle or simple plastic one) and may suffer dehydration, also often leading to a medication build-up in one's system.

Questions to ask your doctor

Before passively accepting a medication and allowing extraneous molecules into your body, a few pertinent questions for your doctor will not go astray.

- *Is it safe for me to take this drug?*
  It is entirely reasonable to ask if the suggested medication is in fact indicated in the first place. A treatment may be intended to address a new symptom or to optimise

---

6   Simon Royal et al., 'Interventions in Primary Care to Reduce Medication Related Adverse Events and Hospital Admissions: Systematic Review and Meta-analysis', *Quality and Safety in Healthcare*, Vol. 15, No. 1 (2006), pp. 23–31.

management of an existing disease, or may be a preventive intervention to lower cholesterol or reduce blood pressure. You can also ask a local pharmacist as to whether or not there are any drug-to-drug interactions or contraindications for the medication combination you have been advised to be on (or even find out over the internet) – and if there are, tell your doctor. That should, in theory, make him or her reflect on the necessity of the prescription in the first place.

- *Have you started me on a low dose?*
  The starting dose should always adhere to the maxim 'start low and go slow' as the substance is gradually introduced and carefully and slowly titrated to produce the intended beneficial effect.

- *How long do you think I will need to take it?*
  Many older patients remain on medication for a very long time, if not indefinitely, and whilst this may be appropriate in some cases, such as for blood pressure medication (antihypertensive agents), in others dose can comfortably be reduced over time. Many prescribers do not want to see their patients indefinitely chained to their pills, yet are anxious about stopping treatment, should the original problem recur.

- *How will you assess the effects?*
  If side effects occur, or are suspected, a thorough review of all medicines is indicated. Dizziness or falling, for example, may be corrected by reducing or stopping medications designed to lower blood pressure. If daytime sedation is experienced when taking sleeping tablets or anti-anxiety medications, these should be cautiously and gradually

reduced, if possible. Caution should be advised, however, if sleeping medications have been taken for many years or even decades and the hypnotic agent or sleeping tablet belongs to the benzodiazepine family of drugs. Coming off these medicines too quickly can be associated not only with rebound insomnia, which can be severe, but also anxiety, agitation, mood changes and even seizures. People are often very fearful about being deprived of their sleeping potion, as very often they will have attempted to reduce the dose by themselves and have failed. The trick here is to reduce at a snail's pace, over months if necessary, and if this causes too much distress, then maintenance treatment at a low dosage may be reasonable – at least the side effects are likely to be less.

Drugs such as antidepressants, antipsychotics or mood stabilisers, which are often intended for long-term use, may still continue to be prescribed even when the patient has had no psychiatric symptoms for years. It may seem feasible and, indeed, prudent, for a doctor to reduce or discontinue these. However, I would issue a word of caution in such circumstances, as I have seen drastic undesirable effects when even a very low or 'micro' dose of a psychotropic medication is abruptly withdrawn. I have a lot more to say about this in the next section of this book.

Stuck on statins?

Some medications achieve the exalted status of being deemed almost worthy of adding to the urban water supply and, indeed, statins seem to fit the bill in this regard. Having being touted as the great protector and cleanser of all blood vessels in the body, their use in older people has grown exponentially. While statin therapy has been shown to reduce first-episode cardiovascular events, and even recurrent ones, there is little evidence that they can ameliorate symptoms associated with mini-stroke changes in the brain or prevent vascular dementia, for example. Many a person presenting with 'muscle cramps' and 'arthritis' has been surprised to learn that this may be a relatively common side effect of statins, as can an increase in liver enzymes – which implies that the liver may not be able to break down other medications as effectively, leading to drug-to-drug interactions and increased levels of other agents in the body. There have also been some reports of cognitive decline with use of statins, although thankfully it is reversible and the evidence for it is not strong.

To market statins effectively, drug companies have had to convince the public of the dangers of high cholesterol in the blood. So now a lot of people, particularly in the US, are highly aware of the difference between 'good' and 'bad' cholesterol and even become obsessively familiar with their own cholesterol levels. But, arguably, the quick fix of lazily consuming a medication can be less helpful than making the therapeutic lifestyle changes, such as good diet and sufficient exercise, necessary to control one's cholesterol levels. Even if one's risk profile for cardiovascular disease is high, it is not clear whether taking statins confers any additional benefit for people in advanced old age (85 plus) or if they simply slot into the perpetual prescribing reflex, whereby repeat prescriptions are filled and the drugs ingested, without further query as to necessity or safety.

Be skilled with the pills

- Get your medications reviewed regularly: this is an important way that we can avoid risk to our health in later life. Being assertive and knowledgeable about every tablet we take is essential.

- Keep a list on you at all times of the medicines you take so that you can impart this crucial information to any health professional you encounter in either a routine or emergency scenario.
- Note any side effects and tell your doctor.
- Make sure you know which medicines are essential for you to take and even dangerous to omit, such as anti-diabetic drugs, anti-epileptic medicines or blood thinners. Aids to remembering include having tablets dispensed in blister packs or dosset boxes, which arrange the tablets in daily compartments. This reduces the risk of forgetting to take the tablets or of 'doubling-up' by accident.
- Treat over-the-counter or non-prescription medicines and even natural remedies in the same way as regular treatments. They still comprise chemicals, after all, and may have side effects and interactions with other medicines, so your doctor needs to know *everything* that you are taking, even if self-initiated and administered. St John's wort (often used for mild depression) is known to interact with blood-thinning medication, for example. Remember that most are for short-term use only, and persistent symptoms of any kind need review and possibly further investigation by your doctor.

Old age is not an illness

We now realise that many of the 'inevitable' symptoms supposedly associated with later life are in fact due to specific treatable conditions and not inherent to old age itself. While growing older is not necessarily about developing sickness and frailty, our chances of developing certain illnesses or conditions do increase. Yet, even though people aged 75 and over are the heaviest users of medical services in developed countries, the absolute numbers in full-time residential or hospital care are small.

Despite some decline in organ and tissue functioning, most of the symptoms and disabilities affecting older people result from disease – yet most laypeople and, sadly, some health professionals still see failing faculties, severe disability and multiple aches and pains as preordained and irreversible concomitants of ageing. A 40-year-old male who calls 999 having experienced chest pain is likely to receive urgent medical assistance, whereas an 85-year-old woman with the same symptom may shrug her shoulders and not even bother to request emergency help or even an urgent home visit from her doctor, as she philosophically attributes these complaints to her advanced age.

I have mentioned that one reason for the establishment of care services dedicated to the needs of older people was the different ways in which illness may present (another was the widespread neglect of older people by the health services down through the ages). A younger person experiencing a chest infection may volunteer 'classic' symptoms such as a cough or shortness of breath but in an older person an infection may present with drowsiness, reduced mobility and even falls and other non-specific symptoms such as reduced appetite without any of the usual tell-tale signs such as a high temperature. Bladder or urinary tract infections (UTIs) may present with symptoms very distant from the site of infection, such as confusion and lethargy. As mentioned earlier, there is an old saying in medicine for older people that atypical modes of presentation are in fact the norm!

So it is vital that the general public and clinicians alike appreciate the differential effects of ageing and illness, especially in its emergency presentations, to avoid disastrous consequences both for individuals and for over-stretched acute medical and emergency services.

Needs, but not must

It is sadly the case that older people may be denied access to many specialised therapies purely because of their age. Although the prevalence of many conditions rises as we age, and older people particularly benefit from specialist services and high-technology procedures, older patients may not receive their fair share of resources when it comes to interventions such as specialist cancer care, renal dialysis and many other treatments. Even cardiopulmonary resuscitation (CPR) in hospital may be withheld (often without discussion with the person or their family) if a member of the medical team, who may in fact have little overall knowledge of the person and their quality of life, judges the prospects of survival as slim. It could be said, therefore, that blatant ageism is rampant in many healthcare systems.

There is no doubt that disability and dependence due to frail health cost the state dearly in terms of resources, and we know that the majority of us will consume the lion's share of health resources in the last year of life, yet it is very difficult to predict when this 'terminal year' has commenced. Although in their present form most healthcare systems, such as services organised and delivered by the HSE in Ireland or the NHS in the UK, prohibit rationing on age criteria, it is still widespread – often during times of crisis in the midst of a winter influenza epidemic, for example. Older people may also be denied access to intensive treatments on a 'fair innings' argument – in other words, after a certain age, you have had your 'share' of world resources and should back off so that younger people can take precedence. It is interesting to see how often older people also subscribe to this dubious philosophy and forgo any claim to costly, intensive but potentially beneficial treatments.

Hospital is no haven

It could be easy to delude oneself into thinking that acute hospitals are sanctuaries where every imaginable ailment affecting the older body will be soothed away. Alas, the reality is more akin to an airport baggage carousel, where unloaded suitcases are haphazardly dumped onto the conveyor belt at their destination, and returned to their owners more scuffed and battered than at the start of the journey. Isn't it also amazing how those bags containing the most essential items for your journey can simply disappear! People of all ages might be equally amazed how often important belongings such as spectacles, mobile phones, purses and wallets and, of course, the essential false teeth go missing in action within the four walls of the infirmary. False teeth, or the set we wished we were born with, have traditionally been the butt of many a hospital gag but their loss can be especially problematic for their owner, when mislaid in the system. Ill-fitting replacements can take weeks or months to get used to and, without one's trusty choppers, it may be impossible to chew and digest hospital rations, quite literally putting the vulnerable patient at risk of malnutrition, as they attempt to recover from acute or chronic illness.

And that brings us on to … the food. It was Hippocrates, the founding father of medicine, who allegedly uttered, 'Let food be thy medicine and medicine be thy food'. Good food should be seen as an integral part of one's hospital treatment. Yet hospital fare has a deserved reputation for frequently being processed (as opposed to fresh) and of dubious quality, served at the wrong temperature and at the wrong times (for example, hospital breakfasts served up at cock crow and 'lunch' arriving before midday). Older patients who are acutely ill may need assistance with eating, and it is intensely distressing and frustrating for families to find their loved one fading away, their food uneaten, just because the ward lacks the staff to help people consume their meals at their own pace. Some more enlightened facilities are, at least, trying to ban medical ward rounds during patient mealtimes, at least preventing the food from going cold – especially as the bedside manner of some medics, who themselves hungrily crave much needed refuelling, can be distinctly lukewarm.

Some sections of acute hospitals may be downright inhospitable and even potentially dangerous for older people. Areas where older patients are treated, be they acute wards or departments such as A & E, may be uncomfortable, noisy, disorientating and completely lack dignity and privacy. There is also a significant risk of picking up an infection whilst in an acute hospital and, should this occur, it may be more difficult to treat, due to a higher prevalence of antibiotic-resistant bacterial strains. Pressure sores are a common complication of prolonged periods of immobility or unduly long waiting times. Also, falls and drug reactions account for considerable morbidity and mortality amongst older patients.

Coupled with the potential 5 per cent loss of muscle strength suffered for every day of treatment in a hospital bed, there is a real risk that the older person can emerge a lot weaker after hospital treatment than before it. All in all, it seems as if patients are shoved through a funnel for the convenience of the institution, rather than the hospital realising its aspirations for patient-centred care.

It takes longer than you might think for an older person to make a full recovery. Unfortunately, a polite and reasonable request for a week or two's convalescence to regain one's strength is likely to be met with a stupefied stare or a mini-lecture from healthcare staff about scarce resources and the need to reserve beds for the sickest of the sick. Florence Nightingale knew about keeping her charges safe while

Mother Nature did the real healing, but today's healthcare systems are about a quick-fire turnover of that most precious commodity in society today: the acute hospital bed.

Statistics from a 2016 report from the UK's National Audit Office revealed that the average length of stay of older patients in acute hospitals is a mere 11.9 days, yet hospitals still remain under pressure to expedite discharge as rapidly as possible.[7] I have personally heard of many instances where relatives and taxis have been phoned at 3 a.m. to assist in the discharge of an older patient from hospital, when pressures from A & E to find a bed to admit another person become overwhelming. Sleep deprivation, which is also an inevitable element of the hospital routine, can persist right up to the point of exit from an acute hospital setting. So I cannot imagine how any meaningful discharge or follow-up plan can be communicated to patients, or those who care for them, in these circumstances.

The truth is that, while full recovery may take a little longer for older people, they *can* recover, given time, just as well as younger peers. But time is a luxury and an essential dignity health services seem unwilling to extend to sick or frail older people. Yet the stakes, in fact, couldn't be higher for those who precariously struggle with independent living. If a discharge is made too early and fails, the spectre of institutional long-term care appears on a rapidly approaching horizon, even if this is contrary to the wishes of the individual. Vulnerable older people too often succumb to the 'advice' of risk-averse clinicians and family members, and quietly withdraw, ostensibly for their own well-being and safety, to the fringes of society in anonymous care facilities and nursing homes.

---

7   National Audit Office, *Discharging Older Patients from Hospital*, London: National Audit Office, 2016, p. 7.

The importance of our environment

The ideal living environment is one that is inclusive, promotes participation and provides space for everyone, including older people. When thinking about older people in this respect, we may tend to focus on the negatives of poor quality environments, communities and deprivation in general, fuelled by excessive media focus on crime; but what about models of optimal inclusion wherein people can achieve personal mastery over life challenges and meet many, if not most, emotional needs? There is no denying the stunting effect of poverty and structural disadvantage; however, we can't assume that all older people are impoverished or dependent or voiceless when it comes to needing essential supports and services.

For many older people, maintaining a home has always been a key life goal and aspiration, from securing and repaying a mortgage if purchased privately, or making renovations according to family requirements. But upkeep of one's home can become a major challenge as we age, and external support may be necessary to maintain independent living. The environment we live in is more than the 'bricks and mortar' of our dwellings but instead encompasses a whole range of facilities, services and professionals that may or may not be essential or available to older people to ensure we thrive, rather merely survive, in later life.

It may sound simplistic to state that almost any human disability, physical or psychological, can be accommodated for if the environment is right, yet there is more than a grain of truth to this statement. Mobility difficulties, in particular, can pose serious problems for an older adult whose home has not been modified appropriately, as this can make daily living tasks and access outside the home challenging. This may have significant knock-on effects in relation to loneliness and isolation. Older properties may become unsafe for those who cannot safely navigate stairs to access an upstairs toilet and who can't afford a stair-lift. Older family properties may also be expensive to heat and keep up or become unkempt, exuding a drab and depressing mood, or have gardens that are difficult to maintain in good condition.

It is good advice to review dispassionately the suitability of your own piece of the built environment and, with an objective eye, try to ascertain if it is future proofed. One's home may be one's castle, but not so much if the sanctuary offered within dwindles to a small portion of the property, namely one or two well lived-in rooms, with close proximity and access to key electrical appliances such as the kettle and the television.

For those with failing memory and for whom moving away from familiar surroundings is inadvisable due to fear of inducing a sense of disorientation, the environment can be made more suitable through labelling, on the outside, the contents of cupboards, cabinets and drawers, and creating a 'memory zone' – a dedicated, highly visible area in one's home, such as a countertop or hall table, with a tray for key possessions, such as keys, phones and wallets, and accompanying wall space on which to hang memory aids such as a whiteboard and date clock.

Mobility impairments may also call for simple, common-sense adaptations to the home, such as moving electrical sockets to a higher level or making cupboards and cabinets less difficult to reach. Many domestic accidents, of course, may be averted by removing slip hazards such as rugs or electrical cables and installing grab rails near a bath or stairs. The benefit of such modifications may seem utterly self-evident but the real tragedy is that they are frequently implemented only *after* an accident or fall, when the metaphorical horse has already bolted, throwing and badly injuring the rider in the process.

It is also time to look at the practical application of science in the home of every older person as, quite clearly, advanced technology has not yet been fully mobilised to make homes age friendly. It is already possible to have imaging sensors in the floor, which can detect when an occupant falls, or technology that can register when a person is sitting in a chair and no longer moving. It will be possible in the near future for older people to communicate with caregivers or family via holographic technology. In-screen 3D holograms are coming soon to our smartphones, making us *feel* that we are with others in the same place, allowing at least partial face-to-face interaction and better quality observation of vulnerable people in their own homes.

We already have the technology through GPS to detect wandering behaviour, through wearable devices which can also monitor temperature, pulse, falls and sleep patterns (although the take-up rate is low, with exception of pendant alarms, which are well established). Why couldn't their use be expanded to enable monitoring of vital signs, such as pulse, or to issue reminders about the need to take medication? This could be transformative for those experiencing memory loss or dementia and reduce the need for visits from outside carers. While people of all ages order food, groceries and other supplies online for convenience, what about smarter homes with all the above, plus voice-activated controls for monitoring and replenishing crucial supplies, such as home heating oil or supplies of medicinal products? If technology can really make living arrangements future-proof and it is available, then why is 'agile ageing' to assist the independent living potential of older people not yet mainstream?

Of course, no smart home can substitute for human interaction. There may also still be many barriers to using what technology is available, as not everyone is tech-savvy and many seniors worry that it will be too complicated for them to learn to use, or that they will somehow break the expensive equipment.

The outdoor environment

There are so many ways in which the outdoor environment has an effect on the quality of life for older people, such as possibilities for meeting people, socialising, building a sense of community, escape from isolation indoors and enhanced feelings of independence. Even just seeing a green outdoor view can aid recovery from surgery,[8] while research has long shown that getting outdoors offers clear physical, social and psychological benefits for older people. For instance, supportive outdoor spaces have been shown to contribute to a more active lifestyle and better physical and mental health, as well as optimal quality of life and life satisfaction. Contact with nature particularly has been shown to reduce mental fatigue, thus aiding in the restoration of a person's ability to concentrate and pay attention, increasing positive mood states, reducing stress and enhancing ability to take things calmly and reflect – an emotional need of increasing importance as we grow older.

However, the inaccessibility and other difficulties presented by many outdoor environments is a major obstacle in preventing people from fully meeting their needs in later life. Practical barriers and hindrances that influence older people in their decision to participate, or not, in outdoor activities include bad or poorly maintained pavements, a fear of crime

---

8   Roger S. Ulrich, 'View Through a Window May Influence Recovery from Surgery,' *Science*, Vol. 224, No. 4647 (1984), pp. 420–1.

or of undesirable gangs, distances that have to be travelled to get to shops and other public services, a lack of benches and a dearth of public toilets. In addition, there may well be speeding vehicles and poorly parked cars, which make crossing the street decidedly hazardous.

I really believe that, unless we play our part in calling for structural deficiencies in the built outdoor environment to be remedied and a greater awareness of the kind of design features that can support independent activities or connection, we are colluding in the attrition and stripping of the independence and dignity of an entire generation, effectively trapping them indoors. It is not an impossible ask. Suffolk Mind, part of the national UK charity Mind, has become so well-known and respected within the UK county of Suffolk that it was asked to contribute to a local supplementary planning guidance document, which will be consulted whenever new developments are proposed. The idea was to take into account town users' mental as well as physical needs. Among the proposals they provided were for some public benches to be semi-circular and placed in a semi-circle, to encourage users to interact with each other, and visual guides to common destinations, such as attractively coloured paving stones leading right to the spot.[9]

Age-friendly environments

Age-friendly environments implicitly acknowledge that older people play a crucial role in their communities by engaging in paid or voluntary work, transmitting experience and knowledge or by helping their families with caring responsibilities. The World Health Organisation's age-friendly cities guide highlights up to eight domains that

---

9   Jon Neal, 'The Mental Health Continuum: Spreading the Message', *Human Givens*, Vol. 25, No. 1 (2018), pp. 16–21.

communities need to address to better adapt not only their physical structures but also their services to meet the needs of older people. These include social participation, respect and social inclusion, civic participation and employment, communication and community support and health services, as well as the quality of the built landscape in which older people reside. Such safe and inclusive spaces for older people to thrive in later years may even prevent or delay the onset of illness and functional decline.

Thankfully, there are notable examples of age-friendly communities, across the developed world primarily, where local officials have taken initiatives to meet such criteria for age friendliness. These include Charleville, County Cork in Ireland, Bilbao in Spain, Manchester in the UK, Utrecht in Holland and Madison, Wisconsin, in the United States. We cannot all move en masse to these places in our later years, so we need to do what we can to make our own locality more age affirming.

Combating loneliness

Taking steps such as the above may go some way towards preventing the social isolation that can make older age such a misery for many people. Undoubtedly, one of our important needs throughout life is for connection. We are all wired for it, to love and be accepted by others, yet external factors such as poverty, violence, discrimination, isolation and loneliness can really undermine the well-being of people at every stage of life. And it isn't just that. As it is now very commonplace, if not the norm, for both parents to work and with many children in crèches, school or day-care, neighbourhoods may seem more like ghost estates rather than a shared suburbia, which embraced multiple generations in the past. Adult children and their families also disperse more readily and geographically more widely than ever before and, with smaller family sizes, the chances of having physical contact with parents and loved ones plummets.

It has been estimated that nine million adults of all ages experience chronic loneliness – more than the entire number of inhabitants of Greater London. We know that loneliness tends to peak at two distinct phases in life, namely during younger and later adulthood. Causes of loneliness in later life may seem fairly obvious, provoked particularly by loss of social networks that can come with retirement, bereavements, mobility problems and other points of transition in our lives.

Less expected, though, were the concerning findings of a report published in December 2017 by the Jo Cox Commission in the UK.[10] More than a third of older people aged 75 and over who responded to the survey endorsed the statement that their feelings of loneliness were out of their control.

Research has revealed that loneliness is bad not just for mental health but has adverse effects on physical health too, increasing the risk of developing coronary heart disease, stroke and elevating the likelihood of early mortality by 26 per cent. To put this into context, chronic loneliness is as bad for our health as smoking fifteen cigarettes per day and is more damaging than obesity.

Loneliness seems to have a direct impact on the immune system, which, when perceiving the body as under attack, primes the body to stave off infection. One of the 'tools' of the immune system is acute inflammation. However, when there is nothing to attack, the result can be a heightened level of chronic inflammation, which is associated with increased risk of developing illnesses such as cancer, heart disease,

---

10 Kate Jopling, *Combatting Loneliness One Conversation at a Time: A Call to Action*, London: Jo Cox Commission on Loneliness, 2017.

Alzheimer's disease or other forms of dementia and major depressive disorder.

People who experience loneliness tend to become more socially risk averse and withdrawn, the very opposite of what our need for connection should be driving us towards. Clearly, if we consider loneliness a form of social hunger, then the only way out of this negative emotional state is to feed our social self and to reconnect with others.

Disclosing loneliness may be extremely embarrassing for many older people, so giving them a sense that it is an entirely legitimate health topic to raise with their GP is crucial in breaking the stigmatised silence around human isolation and its negative effects. Helping older people meet their needs for attention and social interaction can be done formally and informally by health professionals through 'social prescribing'. This may take the form of encouraging participation in task or activity groups where participants share common interests, with the aim of enhancing confidence, social skills and developing satisfying and meaningful relationships.

We cannot assume that this will be the magic solution for everyone, however. Some older people carry unresolved baggage into their later years, such as an inability to trust others, or are scarred from an earlier traumatic experience that has dented their faith in the sincerity of others. Others find it an immense strain to initiate casual conversation or small talk, which is often the prelude to more meaningful social connection. People of all ages may yearn for intimacy yet, as we grow older, we may lose confidence or become deskilled in rapport building with others. The tragedy is that many people with similar needs are on our doorsteps but simply fail to connect – after all, not everyone is a fan of active retirement or voluntary groups and many avoid such networks, believing they will be unable to penetrate the cliques of people they will inevitably encounter.

Some retirees may fail to make new friends through a deep-seated deficit in self-esteem, which may have been 'papered over' by a job or career title which earned them social status and respect from others, but which has now been lost through retirement. Others will have experienced cumulative losses of friends and family over many years and feel that replenishing a network of friends and peers is just too much effort, or doing so will leave them vulnerable again to further hurt and loss.

While there is clearly an onus on older people to participate in and to remain engaged and enthusiastic when it comes to activities and interests in later life, it can be all too easy to fall behind in the context of inevitable losses, health changes and attrition of support networks. The role of local authorities and services is, therefore, key to destigmatise loneliness and signpost people to local sources of support and contact. Barriers to reconnection may also best be understood at community level and investment is required in befriending schemes to assist those most vulnerable to isolation in their own homes, namely those with impaired mobility. If professionals such as GPs emphasise the benefits of 'social prescribing' or referring people to non-medical sources of support within their communities, older people are more likely to engage actively in improving their physical, emotional and mental well-being by tackling loneliness.

Suitable places to live in later life

No discussion of environments would be complete without reference to the range of housing options that older people may need access to. Older people's accommodation options can range from continued independent residence in their communities of origin, through supported living, where the individual has an independent living unit but with some communal services and available care, to full residential or nursing home care. Generally older people do best living with people of diverse ages, where they still have a role and a contribution to make. Novel schemes whereby older people share their home with younger people in exchange for company, care or practical support are increasingly commonplace and promote effective use of their living space, reducing the number of rooms in a home that are unused or dormant. Incentivisation of such schemes by governments could significantly ameliorate the housing shortage that has plagued cities like Dublin, which has witnessed an exponential demand for housing in recent years.

Turning one's home into an asset for the benefit of the older person and a member of the younger generation helps dispel the growing, and already mentioned, societal prejudice that older people are 'blocking' homes by staying in family dwellings no longer entirely appropriate to their needs.

But, if it is simply no longer possible to 'age in place' and the need for assistance outpaces available resources and ability, it may be necessary to consider a move to a continuing care facility.

Choosing care facilities

Choosing a residential or nursing home is one decision that no one wants to get wrong. It is important to recognise that, even if an older person has decided of their own volition to 'check in' to a care facility, the transition can be difficult for all involved. The reality is that a person in these circumstances will be experiencing a loss – a symbolic loss of independence and hopes and dreams for the future. Any outstanding life goals now may seem finally unrealisable and the accompanying sadness this realisation brings may take time to process. Routines and tradition, which unite families in a shared history, may be under severe threat in the new environment, where the personal stories of the residents seem irrelevant to the tasks and requirements of the care facility, in caring for dozens of people.

If the decision is not voluntary and admission to a nursing or care home is directly or indirectly triggered by severe health issues, the older person may see the whole process as being forced upon them and view it as a form of terminal care, rather than later-life support, assuming that their mortality is imminent.

It is important to be aware that temporary depression can set in, as people shrink inwards. This needs keeping an eye on, to ensure this is, indeed, a temporary emotional state, which usually begins to clear in three to five weeks. It can be a necessary state, allowing time for reflection and recalibration of one's lifestyle and ultimately allowing adjustment to a different routine. It is crucial, nonetheless, that friends and family do their utmost to keep the person included in and connected to everyday affairs outside the care home.

It is most helpful if one's own room in the home is personalised as far as possible, with familiar furniture, photos, bed linen and other possessions, to avoid the new resident feeling that they are trespassing in, or confined to, a room that doesn't belong to them. Above all, it is to be hoped that care staff will look at and make use of wider understandings about that person's life, with the sincere objective of tailoring care towards individual preferences and routines. The goal should be to maximise independence, irrespective of how dependent an individual might appear at first.

If the initial depression still persists after some weeks, however, it may indicate a more pervasive clinical depression that warrants treatment.

First impressions and questions to ask

Before it gets anywhere near this point, it can be a useful exercise to make a list of the ideal attributes that you, or your family member, might want from a nursing or care home. This will arm you with your own questions to ask when first going to look around.

Be conscious of first impressions but don't rush to judgement.

Helpful questions to ask include the following, but not all will be relevant for everyone:

- Do the gardens look well maintained?
- Is the home clean and tidy and does it smell nice?
- What is the food like? Having an inspection visit at mealtimes may seem impertinent but it can reveal a lot about the variety, choice and quality of the fare on offer.
- Does the home offer a detailed pre-admission assessment, recording essential information such as a person's personal life story, as well as likes and dislikes?
- Are the staff spontaneous and cheerful or rushed and task focused, and do they allow individual choice when it comes to getting up in the mornings and/or having meals?
- Is there access to a landline phone and a good internet connection?
- Is there a good range of leisure and therapy activities? The ability to do arts and crafts or even creative writing can immeasurably improve the lived experience for residents.
- Are there enough nursing, care and ancillary staff?
- Is there ready access to health professionals such as physiotherapists, speech therapists, dieticians and other specialists?
- Has the home a dedicated general practitioner and how frequently do they visit the home?

- Is the taking of medication supervised?
- Are there established links with community health services and dedicated hospital clinics for older people, which the home has access to?
- Is the staff rostered and available to accompany residents to clinics or does this responsibility fall on family members, if appointments predate entry to the home?
- Are additional charges payable for services such as hairdressing (and speaking of this vital service does the home have its own hairdresser?), massage/manicure or even essentials such as dentistry, chiropody and opticians appointments?
- Are continence aids and dressings available free of cost to each resident?
- Does the home have its own transport for ferrying residents to outpatient appointments or on outings?
- Does the home organise special celebrations for birthdays or anniversaries?
- Does the home schedule regular visits from music and other entertainment groups, pet therapy visits and visits from other voluntary groups?
- Are there facilities for couples who choose to enter the care facility at the same time, such as an extra spacious room and storage space for familiar, emotionally significant belongings?
- Are residents permitted to come and go as they choose or is this severely restricted for health and safety reasons?
- Is a range of newspapers provided (a simple way that connections with the outside world can be maintained) or are residents are expected to consume identical editorials irrespective of prior political or ideological allegiances?
- What arrangements are made to allow residents to vote, by either postal ballot or in person, at the nearest polling station?

- Is parking available for visiting family members, and even residents, or is this discouraged?
- Does the home encourage residents to retain a proportion of their pension for discretionary spending and, if so, how is this transparently managed on behalf of its residents?
- Are care staff expressly discouraged from accepting money or tips of any kind from residents and are there formal policies in place about these and other delicate matters?

Informal chats with care workers, both nursing staff and care assistants, about staff turnover and staff satisfaction levels can be revealing in gauging the overall atmosphere in any home. Try to find out how much notice family members and other supporters receive when planned statutory inspections are imminent, and whether their contribution is encouraged or tacitly discouraged.

It is important to find out how nursing homes handle sensitive issues such as end of life care through formal, advanced care planning. It can be powerfully reassuring for a person to know that an ambulance will not be called for each and every medical event, such as an infection, collapse, blackout, or fall, if it can be dealt with safely at the home and this is what the resident wishes, but equally, whilst undignified and invasive measures such as cardiopulmonary resuscitation (CPR) may be forgone by mutual agreement, active medical care and hospital transfer will still be provided for medical issues such as pneumonias or bladder infections. What is vitally important is to elicit the views of the resident where appropriate and not to exclude them from this process out of a sense of misplaced altruism. Any decision on withholding resuscitative measures should always be subject to review in all cases, particularly in the light of changing health status.

Many homes, but by no means all, are shifting their care ethos away from a paternalistic, best-interests approach to principles based, where possible, on the will and preferences of each individual. This 'pro-choice' approach respects autonomy and even allows an appropriate degree of risk to be borne by the person in respect of daily life choices and decisions – such as when a person declines, for example, to have a care assistant with them while showering or bathing.

Maximising the autonomy of the individual, I believe, will be at the core of delivering high-quality residential care in the future and will be increasingly demanded by more vocal and discerning older consumers of health care. More than that, assigning appropriate roles and tasks to nursing home residents, such as watering plants, or performing reception duties, such as answering the door or phone or relaying messages, can both prevent functional decline and exemplify a greater recognition of the unique emotional needs of each individual – for a sense of autonomy and control, status, achievement and feeling needed. Doing whatever can most help people meet such needs in institutional settings, such as nursing homes, is vitally important. Failure to do so can only produce more rapid disability and decline than would otherwise have occurred.

Mental health

Depression
I have mentioned depression, which is the main form of mental ill health affecting older people, a number of times in preceding pages. Shockingly, under-diagnosis of depression is widespread among older people, although research shows that depression is more frequently experienced by older women,

older people with functionally limiting health conditions and by those living in poverty. When depression takes hold, few emotional needs are likely to stay well met.

Only 20 per cent of older people with major depressive disorder receive effective treatment, according to one primary care survey.[11] Clinicians may dismiss depression as being 'understandable', given the presence of physical illness or a recent loss, such as bereavement. Losses may even appear to stack up and accumulate, each threatening to chip away at psychological defences. It is hard to categorise the breadth and scope of losses that can accompany later life but they may include loss of health, bereavement (loss of companions/ spouses and life partners, friends and family members), loss of material security, loss of role and independence, and loss of mobility and sensory function. The valued social roles that people generally enjoy during their life course are in contrast to the devalued roles that many older adults view themselves as taking on in later life, such as those of medical patient or care recipient.

Other losses that perhaps receive less, or even scant, attention in later life include loss of one's youth, one's parents and loss of fundamental belief systems or faith in institutions through disillusionment or adverse events, when expectations were not matched by experience. An unsympathetic encounter with a health professional, for example, may represent an instance of how our faith in a service or an institution may be blown apart. In relation to loss of health and vitality, it has been stated that many older people experience the loss of pieces of themselves, in that chronic illnesses are very common and, although they may not be immediately life threatening, they can limit function and affect self-image significantly.

---

11 Mijung Park and Jürgen Unützer, 'Geriatric Depression in Primary Care', *The Psychiatric Clinics of North America*, Vol. 34, No. 2 (2011), pp. 469–87.

Picking through the diagnosis of depression

Older people may themselves be reluctant to disclose depressive symptoms, perhaps out of shame, preferring to discuss physical rather than emotional matters with their doctor. One can well imagine a busy GP with a waiting room full of patients and just ten minutes or less to give to each of them not exactly giving top priority to emotional issues and, perhaps inadvertently, even discouraging such dialogue. If the perpetually stressed family physician also believes that depression is inevitable, or that hope of change in a person's situation is futile, then it is easy to see why issues such as major depression are sidelined, and older people continue to suffer.

Diagnosing mental illness in an older person requires no less patience, time and skill than performing a delicate operation or surgical procedure. When a person becomes more hostile or irritable or drinks to excess, a probing beneath the surface may be warranted, as these behaviours, as well as features such as memory impairment or excessive bodily preoccupations, can be signs of late-life depressive illness. Anxiety may be the most prominent feature of depression in older people, which should trigger a psychological enquiry. And self-harm in an older person may take the form of 'giving up' on important aspects of self-care, such as taking blood thinning medication or correctly complying with anti-diabetic treatment.

Psychological conditions such as depression are also underestimated in terms of severity; standard diagnostic classifications categorise them as either major or minor, depending on the presence or absence of certain symptoms. The stark reality is that psychological problems of *any* severity can significantly affect every aspect of the self-care and daily functioning of an older person. Symptoms should never be seen as 'normal' at a certain age, or as an 'understandable' reaction to the stresses and strains of everyday life, as to do so is to dismiss the seriousness of human suffering. Respectful observation, availability of family, friends or health care providers, along with caring support, may indeed be all that is needed when symptoms are largely the consequence of losses, such as bereavement, for example. Yet depression, even when a clearly identifiable trigger is present, can sometimes escalate into a serious, potentially even life-threatening condition.

Always depressed?

On the other hand, depression can become a convenient catch-all diagnosis for issues that people may be reluctant to admit, such as the stress of living without a romantic partner, 'empty nest syndrome', financial worries and especially grief, although the latter is more socially acceptable for discussion. A bereavement reaction generally elicits a public quota of sympathy – until it is judged as lasting too long, that is, and hints are given to the bereaved that they are being self-indulgent now or that they must 'move on' with their lives. Such common life reactions may masquerade as depression but really they are responses to normal endings in life that have no replacement; being supported in acknowledging these losses at least allows a person to mourn them appropriately, and ultimately to explore and re-invent new ways to be involved in life.

The bias against older people on age grounds may mean that mental health services are often configured to deal with the more public face of mental ill-health in old age, namely dementia, rather than the commoner presentations of later-life mental illness, such as clinical depression. The issue of dementia has arguably come to dominate the agenda of mental well-being and old age, and it tends to ignore the fact that the majority of older people do not have this condition. If we focus only on dementia we may forget to discuss the promotion of mental health and wellness in old age and forget the social and environmental factors that can adversely affect well-being in older age, as we have seen. Failure of health professionals to devote time and energy to diagnosing depression because of a mistaken belief that psychological inquiry can only embarrass older people means that untreated mental distress can be left to impair quality of life, increase mortality from physical illness and significantly increase the rate of suicide in older people.

I look at effective approaches to treating depression and mitigating or managing dementia in the next section of this book.

Memory failings – should we worry?

Going upstairs and forgetting what item you intended to retrieve is, thankfully, a poor indicator of the onset of dementia. Everyone at some point or another omits something from their grocery list or becomes embarrassed by forgetting the name of a person they haven't seen in a while. While there is evidence that cognitive ability peaks in our mid twenties and declines steadily thereafter, this does not mean an inevitable crash landing into the territory of dementia. Not all cognitive abilities decline with age – some may remain remarkably stable or even improve over time. Implicit memory (recalling how to carry out familiar tasks) typically shows little or no decline with age. Short-term memory may decline only very little in older people compared with younger people, while semantic memory (knowing facts such as the names of capital cities or colours), actually tends to improve with age. Older people may also do better than distractible youth on memory for planned future actions and will more reliably carry out the tasks agreed to be undertaken in the future, such as making a phone call at a fixed time every week or watering plants every day.

It is perfectly normal to forget some things as we grow older, yet many people have not heard of more benign forms of memory loss such as age associated memory impairment (AAMI) and they tend anxiously to assume that they are developing Alzheimer's disease, or another form of dementia, when they occasionally fail to remember a familiar name or to recall a word. AAMI is a natural process and doesn't indicate that one is on the slippery slope towards something more pathological. Dementia, a progressive loss of memory and other mental abilities that interfere with a person's everyday activities, does become more prevalent with age, yet the majority of people at the age of 90 will still be cognitively intact.

People tend to attribute memory changes as they get older to the biological effects of ageing itself, but factors such as depression or medical problems that cause concentration difficulties, such as an underactive thyroid gland or vitamin B12 deficiency, are frequently overlooked. We know that cognitive side effects may be caused by a wide variety of medications, such as mood stabilisers, pain medications and anti-epileptic drugs. Some of these medications are essential (such as anti-seizure medication) but older people should be informed about associated cognitive side effects so that they are not misattributed. Alcohol excess and smoking can also depress memory and cognitive ability; modifying these habits can enable deficits in cognition to be reversed or avoided altogether.

A considerable proportion of memory problems experienced by older adults are, in fact, reversible and by definition, therefore, not due to dementia. The causes of temporary memory difficulties are varied and more extensive than those of more permanent memory problems such as in Alzheimer's disease. It is likely that many people would be less anxious about their memory ability and less hypervigilant or self-critical about everyday errors, if they were aware of this. Indeed, it is actually family members or carers, rather than the individuals themselves, who tend to notice the more worrying signs of memory loss, such as repetition of statements, repeatedly asking the same question or time disorientation, which can indicate a potentially serious issue with memory and cognitive function.

Challenges to well-being in later years

The psychological difficulties experienced by older people can range from the practical to the psychosocial to the existential, which fail to neatly fall into a diagnostic classification, medical model or other clearly recognisable category. It is important to state that challenges to mental well-being may arise from factors other than mental illness or disorders. In terms of meeting key emotional needs, mental illness can exist when conditions for positive mental health are not met. My own favourite definition of mental health applicable to older adults is an unusually succinct statement from the usually verbose plethora of academic reports that are found in health promotion literature, this clear example being from a 1997 UK Health Education Authority document which stated:

> Mental health is the emotional and spiritual resilience which allows us to enjoy life and to survive pain, disappointment and sadness. It is a positive sense of well-being and an underlying belief in our own and others' dignity and worth.[12]

---

12 Health Education Authority, *Mental Health Promotion: A Quality Framework*, London: Health Education Authority, 1997.

In even fewer words still, mental health reflects, above all, a life with quality.

A UK survey of the seven key determinants of a good quality of life highlighted the importance of the following:

- Having good social relationships with family, friends and neighbours
- Having social roles and participating in social and voluntary activities, plus other activities/hobbies performed alone
- Having good health and functional ability
- Living in a good home and neighbourhood
- Having a positive outlook and psychological well-being
- Having adequate income
- Maintaining independence and control over one's life.[13]

Pretty well all the primary emotional needs feature in that lot!

The key question to be answered, however, is how people manage to maintain well-being if conditions in their lives are less than desirable. We know that in older age there is an increased likelihood of loss of a spouse or close friends, increasing social isolation and loneliness (one in five older people is alone for more than twelve hours each day). Older people may also experience low income if they rely purely on fixed means such as a state pension, and nearly three-quarters of 85-year-olds have limiting, longstanding illnesses. Some illnesses, such as dementia, even double in prevalence every five years after the age of 65. Mobility issues are particularly common among those aged 85 and older, and such difficulties tend to restrict opportunities for travel as well as compromise

---

13 Ann Bowling et al., 'Let's Ask Them: A National Survey of Definitions of Quality of Life and its Enhancement among People Aged 65 and over', *International Journal of Ageing and Human Development*, Vol. 56, No. 4 (2003), pp. 269–306.

independence and social functioning. Without mobility, one's home can be rendered more akin to a prison.

Thus there are no quick fixes for optimal mental health in older people and ensuring their continued well-being and full participation in society by addressing inequalities, in terms of opportunity, remains crucial.

Getting health challenges into perspective

It must be remembered that not all bodily changes are harbingers of imminent doom and normal ageing can involve hearing and visual loss; loss of muscle and bone mass; decreased sensitivity to touch, smell and taste; loss of skin and muscle elasticity; and slower healing in the face of injury and illness. Not all these changes are inevitable, however, but, along with common illnesses such as arthritis, high blood pressure and cholesterol or osteoporosis, they do occur more frequently in later life. Yet older people regularly report their health as good, in spite of some impairment.

The impact of disability on one's well-being thus seems to depend more on the perception of the situation. Proactive adaptation to and acceptance of a lower level of function are crucial elements of personal resilience, if reduced mobility or other functional impairments do occur. But I want to stress yet again that none of these changes are inevitable in later life and that old age is not an illness.

Contrary to negative stereotyping, changes in cognition are usually not due to dementia and while decline in abilities, such as learning new information or solving novel problems, is fairly usual, other abilities, such as vocabulary span or use and application of accumulated knowledge, actually improve with age.

There is also plenty of evidence that symptoms such as delusional thinking or hallucinatory experiences that may accompany mental illnesses such as schizophrenia earlier in life become less intense in older years. Also, through accumulation of life experience and wisdom, older people may be more resilient to some of the setbacks and stresses of life and so are less vulnerable to resorting to alcohol and illicit drug misuse and the ravages they bring. Problems associated with personality disorders also appear to fizzle out with advancing years.

On occasion, there can be the 'double whammy' of physical and psychological losses occurring simultaneously. The timing of losses can seem arbitrary, random and even almost downright cruel, as no sooner has an individual overcome one challenge than another comes storming along. Equally, losses can sometimes accumulate and stack up on each other, threatening to overwhelm one's coping reserves.

Coping style

We all know instances where both members of a couple fall ill at some point and the roles of patient and carer are unfortunately shared, fluid and interchangeable. Yet coping and resilience at many different levels is frequently observed, often with professional and paid domiciliary care helping to fill gaps in support networks. I personally have found it astounding to witness, when serious losses in physical or mental health occur, how adaptive people can be in assuming the role of caregiver to their partner. I have seen many male caregivers learn to cook, clean and shop for the first time in their later years and seen wives who had never previously handled finances become experts in managing them when their partner develops dementia.

The meaning attached to each loss may be very different and variable, and it is a mistake to assume that all older people will be consumed by loss, pain or disappointment, even if over a given time period the 'balance-sheet' of gains versus losses appears to register in the negative. Maintaining a positive self-image, social participation and ease, and a feeling of belongingness can literally melt away individual losses over time, even those that appear especially salient, such as the death of a spouse. Losses may also be 'staged', in that the grieving process is done over an extended period, with the final passing of a loved one who has experienced a difficult, painful or protracted terminal illness coming even as a relief.

A certain desensitisation to bereavement also seems to occur as one ages, with an acceptance of the inevitability of the loss of siblings, for example. Although each loss may mean our support network is reduced and it may be harder to recruit replacements as we age, the stoicism displayed by many elders in the face of much death and grief is remarkable and instructive for younger generations to witness.

Whatever our circumstances, we can learn how to make the best of them by the way we approach things psychologically. Psychological well-being is a product of life satisfaction and happiness, along with personality resources such as self-esteem, competence, control and resilience, all essential elements of good mental health. These attributes, plus continuing opportunities to play a part in society, may offset other negative aspects of later-life circumstances such as ill health, lack of material resources or functional deficits.

How to keep mentally healthy – audit your needs

The Human Givens framework of emotional and psychological needs, which is the cerebral equivalent of a balanced diet, allows us all to audit our emotional requirements and how well they are being met, and see where we need to take appropriate action – in collaboration, if deemed advantageous, with a suitably qualified therapist, who is expert in this area.

When we think of the term 'audit', taxation, accounting and sterile number-crunching exercises perhaps come to mind. It may be surprising to learn that emotional needs can usefully be audited too and, in a way, taking a dispassionate and number-based view of our inner thoughts and experiences allows for a more objective analysis of what we need to work on. An extremely useful tool called the Emotional Needs Audit is available to download from the Human Givens Institute (www.hgi.org.uk). It is a simple diagnostic questionnaire that measures what is working for us emotionally and what isn't, identifying where we need to consider making changes.

Emotional Needs Audit – (Rate each answer on a scale of 1 to 7 – 1 indicating need is unmet, 3–4 being partially met and 7 indicating a very well met need.)

1. Do you feel secure in all major areas of your life (such as your home, work, environment)?
2. Do you feel you receive enough attention?
3. Do you think you give other people enough attention?
4. Do you feel in control of your life most of the time?
5. Do you feel connected to some part of a wider community?
6. Can you obtain privacy when you need to?
7. Do you feel an emotional connection to others? For instance, do you have an intimate relationship in your life, one where you are totally physically and emotionally accepted for who you are by at least one person (this could be a close friend)?
8. Do you feel you have status that is acknowledged?
9. Are you achieving things and feeling competent in at least one major area of your life?
10. Are you being mentally and/or physically stretched in ways which give you a sense that life is meaningful?

I now invite you to complete your own emotional needs audit according to the above checklist. I suggest you do this when you have time to give it calm consideration and reflection. The questions below will help prompt you in the areas to think about. When you have deliberated, give yourself a score somewhere from 1 (where the particular need is not met at all) to 7 (where you think it is very well met). If your scores are mostly low, you are more likely to be experiencing stress symptoms. If any need is scored 3 or less, this is likely to be a major stressor for you. Even if only one need is marked very low, it can be enough of a problem to seriously threaten your mental and emotional well-being.

Do you feel safe?

- How safe do you feel in your home environment? Are you worried about your personal security either at home or in your neighbourhood?
- Have you been a victim of crime or antisocial behaviour or are you being bullied by anyone – even by someone who should have your welfare as a high priority, such as a spouse, relative or carer?
- Do you feel particularly vulnerable because of health issues and illness or worry about becoming unwell or falling or having an accident at home, and no one knowing about it, so receiving no help?
- Are you struggling to survive financially?
- Are you worried about adverse weather that could see you isolated without vital supplies of food or medicine?

It is hardly surprising that some older people struggle to enjoy any level of optimism when they perceive serious threats to their well-being.

Do you have a sense of autonomy and control?

- Do you have responsibility for making important decisions in your life or do other people have undue influence or power over you?
- Have you recently lost control over crucial issues such as where you are living, perhaps because of illness, which has compromised your ability to live where you would ordinarily wish to be?
- Do you have adult children pressurising you to support them financially or to liquidate or prematurely bestow control over your assets in their favour? Are you denying yourself basic comforts because of ongoing financial obligations to your offspring?
- Do you feel obliged to provide childcare to grandchildren because crèche fees are unaffordable?
- Have adult children returned home to live with you, perhaps because of divorce, but without any willingness to contribute to household bills?

These are some of the many life scenarios that older people may find threatening their ability to direct the course of their own lives.

Do you give and get sufficient attention?

- Many older people lose confidence in their ability to contribute in many areas of life and are reticent about voicing their opinions, let alone their needs. Is this true of you?
- Do you spend a great deal of time on your own or are you dominated by other people, who live with you or visit you, who demand a lot of attention and sap your energy in the process?

- Do you get attention from being depressed or being overly negative, or talking about illness and symptoms a great deal of the time, worrying those who care about you?
- Are you interested in the ideas and experiences of younger people, paying genuine attention to them or do you decline to get involved with their issues, their language and their concerns?
- Do you consider that family members should help you out and meet your needs, to the detriment of their own independence?
- Do you try to draw attention by being deliberately outrageous or provocative rather than being your true self?

In many ways attention needs can be harder to meet as we grow older, requiring creativity and confidence to do so consistently.

Do you enjoy close and intimate relationships with other people?

- Do you have at least one person that you feel very close to, be it a spouse/life partner or very dear friend?
- Have you recently been bereaved and do you feel lonely?
- Have you lost friends, as the years go by, and do you find it hard to replace what they added to your life?
- Do you feel a warm connection with and from family members or do you feel resented and like a burden?
- Have you made any new, important and lasting friendships in the last decade?

Do you have wider connections with others?

- Are you involved with a religious or charitable organisation?
- Do you engage in hobbies or leisure-time activities that bring you into contact with others?
- Do you play a part in local politics?

- Are you involved with a neighbourhood or community organisation?
- Have you relinquished membership of a club, such as golf or bridge, or dropped an adult education class because you can no longer afford expensive membership fees, or because of physical or psychological complaints which stop you attending?
- Can you go days without seeing anyone?

Are you content with your status and how others see you?

- Do you feel suitably appreciated and rewarded for what you do for others – such as caring for grandchildren or caring for a sick spouse?
- How comfortable are you about the gradual signs of ageing in your appearance or do you make huge efforts to hide these, for instance by dyeing your hair, wearing young people's clothing, etc.?
- Do you feel you still have status in society or do you feel dismissed, mocked or invisible as an older person?
- Do you compare yourself to others and experience jealousy, feeling that you could have achieved so much more in life?
- Do you feel that you have sufficient or insufficient material goods to show for years of toil, whether paid or unpaid?

Do you have a sense of competence and achievement?

- Are you doing/planning to do what you want to do in retirement or have any changing and unforeseen circumstances blocked your plans for all those hobbies and interests you intended to cultivate?
- Do you feel that you can no longer dream or set future goals and have to fall back on memories instead?

- Do you get a sense of achievement through voluntary roles in which you help others?
- Do you now question all the energy you put into work and think you could have spent your leisure time more productively?
- Have you had to take on a role you had never done before, such as caring or dealing with the family finances? If so, do you feel you have done this well or that you struggle?
- Have you any outlet remaining for using your professional skills?

Does your life feel meaningful?

- Are you continuing to learn new skills and take on new challenges?
- Do you spend time on things that you think matter – whether that means helping out with the grandchildren, mentoring others in areas of your expertise or campaigning about something you care about?
- Do you like to go the 'extra mile' for others and, in so doing, feel that you make a real difference in their lives?
- Do you feel you have done your bit and now it's your turn to take it easy – and yet you find you feel bored or negative about all the time you have to fill?
- Do you find it difficult to get the motivation to get out of bed in the mornings?
- Do you feel that, once you are older, you are pretty useless or do you feel that others can benefit from what you have learned in your life?

The meeting of our emotional and psychological needs is not a luxury; it is an essential prerequisite to good mental health, well-being and thriving. You may even find, once you have gone through the checklist and given it wide consideration, that your life is going better than you thought and that anxiety or black-and-white thinking has been blowing things up out of proportion. It is helpful to do this quick stocktaking exercise on many occasions, particularly when we have experienced a change of circumstances. It can remind us which kinds of stresses leave us most vulnerable and which forms of resilience and life resources are the most important for getting us through.

Resources unbroken

Some of the resources at our disposal are actually enhanced with the passage of years and the benefit of life experience. The attributes of wisdom, self-efficacy, resilience and environmental mastery may truly only come to the fore as we grow in years. So too does the ability to regulate our emotions better, to accept ourselves for what we are and to prioritise. If our earlier, anxious and younger selves could see how the soothing effects of time melt away many of our fears and forebodings, then more people would surely embrace their later years as a coming to fruition, rather than as a time of decay.

We know from research that the human brain seems to experience dips and rises in happiness levels at different ages, with life satisfaction falling in our twenties and thirties, hitting a trough in our late forties, before increasing until our eighties.[14] It seems that it is not so much the conditions of our lives that determine this shift in outlook but that how we *feel* about our lives seems to change as we approach our later years.

Jonathan Rauch, author of *The Happiness Curve*,[15] claims that some of the greater contentment enjoyed by older people

---

14 David G. Blanchflower and Andrew J. Oswald, 'Is Well-being U-shaped over the Life Cycle?', *Social Science and Medicine*, Vol. 66, No. 8 (2008), pp. 1733–49.

15 Jonathan Rauch, *The Happiness Curve: Why Life Gets Better After 50,* London: Green Tree, 2018.

is due to their entertaining less regret and stress, dwelling less on negative information and being better able to manage their emotions as well as to their ability to 'switch off' status competition, as their values change. It may be simplistic to say that gratitude replaces greed in later years, but perhaps this could helpfully be the aspiration for every would-be maturing older person.

Older age may also be the time when the spiritual aspects of life seem to matter more, allowing us to experience something greater than ourselves and to appreciate simplicity rather than complexity, particularly in the natural environment. A sense of contented discernment, quiet inner satisfaction and self-respect are perhaps the greatest gifts that can emerge as life enters its autumnal phase.

Older age: the silver lining

Many workers who are intuitive, reflective, self-effacing and more introvert in personality style may ultimately taste success in later years, attaining positions of seniority within organisations frequently later in their careers than people who display more overtly extravert personality styles. We may admittedly be the same people on the inside but the ageing process ensures that we accumulate knowledge and experience which, in a world of rapid change, is still likely to be a valuable social and commercial currency.

> John had been a middle-ranking executive at a large insurance company for many years. He had shown enormous loyalty to the organisation over a long period, which had often involved painful changes and upheavals, such as mergers with bigger companies, downsizing and periodic expansions.

John had, through his intuition, empathy and problem-solving skills, contributed to a very positive working atmosphere within his department. By nature, John was a natural communicator with an excellent ability to listen to colleagues' concerns and help them find their way through, matched by an eye for detail and sound judgement in his approach to work, resulting in his contributing good results for the company balance sheet. Yet, throughout his career, however, he felt considerable personal frustration at an inability to contribute to board meetings, and to 'talk-up' these many achievements. He felt anxious about thrusting himself forward, lacking the assertiveness, brashness and loud but hollow passion of his younger male colleagues.

His confidence received a further severe blow when he was persuaded to attend an interview for the position of departmental head but failed to secure the post, as he was judged to have performed poorly at the interview itself. A younger colleague with a reputation for rudeness and ruthlessness obtained the post, to the dismay of John's co-workers. To make matters infinitely worse, John felt taunted by his new boss and became terrified of making a mistake, even when doing familiar and quite routine work.

A dramatic change of fortune occurred for John, however, when his new boss suddenly left the organisation and John was asked to run his section on a temporary basis. Having first hesitated out of wounded pride, he then accepted the post because rising university costs for his two children had become the main issue to consider. Within a few years, John had secured the post on a permanent basis, and gradually found his voice at the management table, becoming ever more comfortable and at ease, especially when his innate talents for nurturing existing customers and maintaining business in the face of stiff competition were recognised by his senior managers.

By the time of his retirement a few years later, John's person-centred approach was so recognised and valued that he was invited to carry on part-time consultancy work with his former employer. There is little doubt that, in many ways, older age was good to John in that loss of anxiety and inhibition ultimately allowed him to achieve key life goals.

Still contributing, still healing

As we become less self-conscious and less inhibited by personal (rather than socially affirmed) feelings of inadequacy, we may have more time to devote to caretaking, nurturing and relaying pearls of wisdom for other generations to cherish. Our gifts and insights may even allow us quietly to compete with people belonging to other age categories and perhaps stay ahead in the social relevance stakes, even if this is not immediately recognised.

The credibility of older people to lead, to apply common sense in solving or ameliorating almost any problem is enhanced by their experience of life's ups and downs. It is the very need of grandparents to connect and contribute, for example, that sees them play such a meaningful role as mentors to children who yearn to be seen, loved and encouraged. As key members of an extended family, older people who apply their resources to the development and well-being of the young in turn meet their own need to be connected to, contribute to and challenged by others.

The significance of *not* having a caring and unconditionally supportive and loving mentor such as a grandparent cannot be overstated, even manifesting in the splintering of family units, a relatively new phenomenon, and can contribute to many problems in society such as school failure, drug abuse and greed. The successful attainment of mutual emotional needs between and across the generations, on the other hand, emphasises the connectedness between people and strengthens the notion that mental thriving is not a solo endeavour but is rather an essential collective activity for human society.

Mind and body health: how to optimise well-being

We now have the evidence that even if measures such as stopping smoking, eating healthily and taking exercise are adopted relatively late in the life cycle, there is benefit. Lifelong couch potatoes who convert and become latter-day 'crouch potatoes' by taking up exercise can make up for at least some lost time, it seems. All this is really important for vascular health (see below). And what is good for physical health is good for mental health.

Get moving

As a society, we tend to have conflicting messages about the ageing body. There is advice in abundance about the medical advantages to staying fit, yet somehow we also get the idea that only gentle exercise is appropriate and indeed all we are capable of past a certain age. Many adults aged 65 and over spend, on average, ten hours or more each day sitting or lying down, making them the most sedentary age group, with just one out of four people aged between 65 and 74 years exercising regularly.

Physical exercise and movement not only helps with balance training, cardiovascular fitness and general mobility but also boosts mood and cognitive performance. Even if pain, overweight, breathlessness or anxiety do reduce the amount of exercise it is wise to do, it is still possible to maintain a degree of fitness, even with health problems. Indeed, later life may be the time to concentrate on getting fit as, after working age, there is more time and opportunity to get hearts pumping and to break into a healthy sweat. But do seek medical advice before starting any fitness programme, to ensure what you're planning on doing is right for you.

It is also best to set sights lower rather than higher, as even a seemingly unambitious regime can be good for one's health and spirits. As that popular maxim of the fitness community puts it, 'No matter how slow you go, you're still lapping the people on the couch.' Gentler methods of exercise such as swimming, aqua aerobics or a brisk walk are fine alternatives to hitting the gym. Equally, for those not intimidated by younger biceps, the challenge of strength training can be usually accommodated, provided one starts slowly and builds from that point.

From an emotional needs perspective, physical exercise is in keeping with the sustenance we derive from food, water and shelter – an essential element of survival and health to be obtained within our environment, to help us stave off the damaging effects of inertia on body and mind. There is a very direct relationship between movement, survival and optimal health. An inactive lifestyle takes a greater toll on the body's athletic ability than biological ageing.

Exercise is easiest to start and maintain when it is *fun*. 'Never Leave the Playground' is the wonderfully named programme of activities that stimulates brain and body strength by specific training of the hands and feet devised by Stephen Jepson.[16] Born in 1941, Jepson is a fitness instructor who originally taught ceramics at the University of Florida but who went on to research and document the benefits of the theory of lifetime fitness. By inventing toys and games akin to those found in a children's playground, Jepson encourages the practice of constant movement through play, as opposed to physical exercise. Demonstration videos show that, irrespective of how impaired through disuse and de-conditioning our bodies have become, we can, though a graded series of exercises and play, become more supple in body, stable in our balance and satisfied in mind. It was George Bernard Shaw who said, 'We don't stop playing because we grow old. We grow old because we stop playing.' Jepson's genius seems to be in the realisation that the fun of play (physical, emotional and intellectual), and not just exercise on its own, is a virtual fountain of youth and continuity.

Learning new physical activities is also likely not only to keep us fit but to enhance neuroplasticity (the creation of extra or surplus neural pathways and cognitive reserve) to keep our minds sharp as well.

Never too late to start

The rather consoling part of turning over a new leaf in relation to physical exercise is the fact that, irrespective of one's age, it's never too late to get started and some movement, any movement, is better than none. Changes made even relatively late in life can be beneficial for your physical condition but also for mind, mood and even memory. It appears that it is the single biggest contributor to longevity. People who exercise tend to have improved immune and digestive functioning, better blood pressure and bone density and a lower risk of Alzheimer's disease, diabetes, heart disease, osteoporosis

---

16 See http://neverleavetheplayground.com.

and certain cancers. Physical health benefits of exercise include improvements in flexibility and posture, reducing the risk of falls by preventing loss of bone and muscle mass. Better muscle strength can alleviate the symptoms of chronic conditions such as arthritis.

Psychological benefits of exercise include improvements in sleep, relief of stress and depression through a boost in endorphins (mood-enhancing brain hormones) and an increase in one's self confidence, through the sense of achievement derived. While the mind gym can be undoubtedly very beneficial for the brain, physical exercise still beats sudoku, crossword puzzles and computer games hands down. Aerobic exercise literally squeezes blood into the frontal lobes of the brain, perfusing tissue which may hitherto have been deprived of oxygenated blood due to progressive narrowing of critical blood vessels as we age.

Staying on track

Starting an exercise routine may entail overcoming obstacles, many of which come from within. Key is setting lifestyle goals that are appropriate for one's age and that fit into a schedule that you can commit to. Activities that are enjoyable can be incorporated into an exercise routine to increase motivation and build in rewards and incentives. Perhaps exercise time can also be social time, through communal activities such as yoga or tai chi.

A balanced exercise plan should address a number of parameters of physical fitness, including working on balance; cardio performance to increase endurance; strength and power to remain active and avoid falls; and flexibility to increase the range of movement for everyday physical activities such as tying laces or playing with grandchildren. Getting started safely and slowly is crucial if exercise is to be sustained and the risk of injury minimised. Committing to an exercise schedule for three to four weeks at the outset is crucial so that it becomes a habit, and inevitably this is easier if enjoyable activities are chosen. Experimenting with mindfulness and focusing on how your body feels as you move, instead of zoning out, is helpful in relieving stress and worry and picking up signs of potential injury at an early stage.

Staying motivated can be challenging if the weather takes a turn for the worse and heading outdoors on dark, cold evenings threatens to rust the joints and hinges of even the strongest, most fanatical senior ironman. So:

- Keep short-term goals in mind, such as reducing stress or making that 10 km walk in under a certain time – with, of course, a healthy reward at the end!
- Keep a log and reach out for support when resolve wavers.
- Plan in advance how you will handle obstacles along the path. For instance, how will you continue your schedule when you're on holiday or when your exercise buddy moves away or if you move to a new community? Equally if you or your partner becomes ill, will it mean an abrupt end to your exercise objectives? Staying on course when that all-important routine changes is challenging for sure, but with creativity and flexibility, it is possible to stay fit, even if you have to take time out to recover from illness or surgery perhaps.

How, what and where to eat

Snacking on the go is one of the many bad habits that may have crept into our eating during our working careers, as we brought home the bacon and perhaps sampled it a bit too often en route. As we retire or gain more time, however, a new-found pleasure can be encountered at the dining table, generating purposeful, healthy eating habits that create new experiences and bring people together.

Since time immemorial, food has united families and communities in cultures around the world. The trick for older people is to bring the act of eating into our lives in a way that enriches our interpersonal relationships and our relationship with food at the same time. The food that we digest is truly greater than the sum of its ingredients. Yet it is all too easy to fall into bad habits around food, especially when it comes to its preparation. It can also seem such an effort to cook for one when you're living alone.

'Virtuous eating' encourages us to carefully consider what we eat, to handle food from raw, and to slowly prepare and consume modest quantities of a range of nutritional ingredients. We know from research such as the CALERIE study, sponsored by America's National Institutes of Health, that calorie restriction brings benefits in terms of human health, not least through preventing conditions such as diabetes.[17] Human metabolism slows as we age, so we need to consume less, or exercise more, to maintain the same body weight.

There may be an even bigger dividend to be obtained, however, potentially reversing conditions such as diabetes, high cholesterol or even heart disease, by consuming more of those foodstuffs that we have long known are good for us, such as whole wheat carbs, vegetables, legumes and low-fat produce. A Mediterranean diet enriched with omega-3 fatty acids, lots of fruit and vegetables may, moreover, be protective against conditions such as dementia and cognitive decline. We can also allow ourselves the occasional treat, such as wine and dark chocolate, which has been reported to prevent arteriosclerosis or progressive hardening of the arteries.

If we are undeniably what we eat, then what, apart from the ingredients, are the rules of engagement around consumption

---

17 See https://calerie.duke.edu.

for good digestion? Eating slowly and mindfully helps us appreciate what we eat, and many cultures around the world would think it sacrilegious to eat on the run. Sitting down at a stylishly laid table, even if you are the only guest, can allow you to appreciate every bite of food and decompress from the stress of the day. It also reminds you that your self-care is important. Perhaps you might even blend in music, a candle and anything else that you might borrow from the ambience of your favourite restaurant to enhance the experience.

Eating with others helps fill our need for connection in a most pleasurable way and encourages us to treat mealtimes as events worth savouring. Such occasions don't have to be formal or pre-planned, but can be just spontaneous and thoroughly social. Food preparation can become stressful if we always aim for perfection and try to outshine those celebrity chefs, but, on the other hand, learning from the professionals and showing off our new found culinary knowledge can really motivate us to take our relationship with food preparation to another level. Aiming to cook one new, easy but healthy meal once a week will help expand one's repertoire of knowledge of convenient but nutritious cooking without leading to a loss of sanity.

Beware of one too many

Alcohol is for many of us a pleasure and a social indulgence, yet an analysis of data from a recent US National Epidemiologic Survey on Alcohol and Related Conditions suggests that one in five people have had a substance or alcohol abuse problem at some point in their lives.[18] The dangers of excessive drinking are clear in terms of liver damage, but much less

---

18 Deborah S. Hasin et al., 'Prevalence, Correlates Disability and Co-morbidity of DSM-IV Alcohol Abuse and Dependence in the United States: Results from the National Epidemiologic Survey on Alcohol and Related Conditions', *Archives of General Psychiatry*, Vol. 64, No. 7 (2007), pp. 830–42.

appreciated is the risk of depression and brain damage from excess alcohol in later years.

How much is too much is always the big question. Despite figures which show that older people drink far less than younger people in terms of weekly units consumed, they have reduced tolerance to the effects of alcohol and are more likely to drink on an almost daily basis over the course of the week. A consensus of opinion seems to agree that adults over the age of 65 should not drink more than seven units (or standard drinks) per week, with no more than three drinks on a given day. This is about half the maximum recommended weekly intake for healthy adults under the age of 65. Exceeding these levels increases the risk of falls, medication interactions and a range of adverse health events. It is also vital to have drink-free days to avoid developing an alcohol habit.

When I am seeing someone for a psychological assessment, if I see that they have a history which might include repeated confusional episodes, falls, recurrent chest infections, bleeding stomach ulcers or heart failure, it always raises my index of suspicion about an underlying alcohol problem. It seems that elderly widowers are the single most vulnerable group in this regard and unless alcohol-related issues are addressed, little progress can be made in treating underlying issues such as depression or anxiety. Fortunately, older drinkers can respond to a range of therapy techniques to deal effectively with addictive issues, especially alcohol use disorders, but being vigilant about the presence of co-existing conditions that can accelerate harmful drinking is important. Alcohol dependency can mask many a problem including depression, anxiety and social isolation to name but a few.

Be vigilant about change

Sometimes it pays to be an inner hypochondriac when it comes to noticing changes in one's body that may represent important symptoms of physical illness. The earlier a serious health condition is diagnosed and understood, the better the prognosis in general. It can pay to notice rapid weight loss, bleeding from anywhere, persistent cough, abdominal pain or unexplained hoarseness, as these some of the must-act indicators that further investigation is required. As a general rule of thumb, if any new and uncomfortable symptom persists for a two-week period or longer, then it's off for a check-up you should go. And don't forget about the value of screening in identifying functional, cognitive, mood, hearing and visual impairments – speak to your doctor, if you are concerned.

Look after your heart and your brain

We need to take vascular disease suitably seriously. Vascular disease, which is disease of the blood vessels supplying the brain, the heart and the extremities such as the lower limbs, is one of the biggest causes of mortality, morbidity and disease in the western world. There is an old saying in public health that a healthy heart is a healthy brain because the same risk factors (such as diabetes, high cholesterol, smoking and high blood pressure) affect both. Our hearts and our brains rely on a very intricate supply of blood flowing through a network of large and smaller vessels, delivering oxygen and other nutriments and removing toxic by-products of cellular metabolism.

In many ways the brain is even more vulnerable than the heart to an interruption of that supply. A clot or a plaque deposit blocking a major artery in the brain can cause a sudden stroke due to immediate death of brain tissue, but more insidious damage can be caused by a reduction in brain blood flow, leading to gradual damage to brain tissue. Such mini-stroke changes to the brain are remarkably common. A scan study, carried out in Rotterdam in 2001, of adults aged between 60 and 90 revealed that 95 per cent of them showed mini-stroke changes in the brain on routine MRI brain scans.[19] Just because this isn't routinely identified doesn't mean that nothing is happening. The changes can be associated with a range of difficulties such as memory and cognitive difficulties and problems with walking and balance.

It is now appreciated that mini-stroke or ischaemic changes in the brain can also contribute to the emergence of Alzheimer's disease and that changes in the brains of people with Alzheimer's (the deposits of plaques and tangles) are more likely to be symptomatic if there are mini-strokes or blood vessel damage also. It is estimated that up to a third of the risk of developing Alzheimer's could be related to such damage and may potentially be avoidable if vascular damage is minimised.

Monitoring and managing our vascular risks is, therefore, essential for brain health in later years and you can't rely on taking blood thinners to increase brain blood flow, as these can be associated with bleeding. There are much better ways to stay healthy.

Increase heart and brain health by:
- Taking sufficient aerobic exercise: this will help increase the flow of blood in our brains
- Keeping blood pressure under control – neither too high nor too low

---

19 Frank-Erik de Leeuw et al., 'Prevalence of Cerebral White Matter Lesions in Elderly People: A Population Based Magnetic Resonance Imaging Study – The Rotterdam Scan Study', *Journal of Neurology, Neurosurgery and Psychiatry*, Vol. 70, No. 1 (2001), pp. 9–14.

- Stopping smoking: smoking narrows and constricts blood vessels everywhere in the body – it is never too late to get benefit from stopping
- Losing weight, if overweight: in addition to being associated with raised cholesterol, overweight increases the risk of diabetes, which also causes damage to blood vessels
- Eating a good and varied diet
- Keeping the brain active.

Our 'mothership', the brain, is the centre not only of our mental well-being and personhood but is also the guardian of our physical health, and we need to be extra vigilant about its state of well-being and integrity as our chronological score grows.

Reduce health hazards in later life

In my experience as a clinician working with older people, I have on countless occasions seen how common health hazards, especially falls, can have a drastic and quite disproportionate effect on older people's lives. It is estimated that, every year, one in three adults aged 65 and older will fall. The physical consequences include broken bones, open and closed head injuries (sometimes even resulting in internal brain bleeds) and bruising, but the psychological effects, such as loss of confidence, social isolation, depression and emotional trauma can be equally severe. Without over-stating the obvious, a simple thing such as a fall can radically change the life of an older person and it behoves health care professionals and therapists of all disciplines to inform and educate about this topic.

- Do a survey of your property to remove obstacles such as clutter, loose rugs and cables; checking the light levels (avoiding dimness or excessive brightness) and raising the level of plugs, sockets and toilet seats can be highly prudent. Far from being seen as a race to the bottom, in terms of expectations of life, I like to think of such preventive acts as practical age-proofing of one's personal environment. In prevention terms, I think this ranks alongside the flu vaccine.

- Pay attention to stairs and bathrooms; these are common fall zones, yet extra rails can make a significant difference in terms of minimising the likelihood of slips and trips.
- While there is not much you can do about external pavements, be observant and vigilant, and avoid rushing in haste or venturing out in bad weather.
- Keep spectacles and hearing aids at the right prescription to help prevent falling.
- Be extra wary if taking medications such as sleeping pills, antidepressants, antipsychotics or drugs to control mood. These can put people at extra risk of falls due to impairment of balance and gait. Equally, people who rely on medication to control high blood pressure may find that they feel dizzy if the medications 'overwork' and lower blood pressure too much – especially likely to happen when someone rises to stand – causing a stumble. Dose reductions may be necessary.
- Take extra care when driving: older drivers face challenges in relation to changing road and motorway configurations, and greater use of dashboard technology. Although driving is a well-learned skill for most of us, we may need to submit ourselves for more frequent on-road assessments to demonstrate our continued competence. We know that although accident rates are often less for older, compared with novice, drivers, certain abilities such as reaction times decline with age and people may need to modify driving

behaviour, especially if medication or memory issues impair concentration and judgement. Perhaps with future self-drive technology, the real race-winners will be older people, who will stay connected with their four wheels for a lot longer!

Go for mind food

We all need to feed our minds – with delicious calm. When the body is truly relaxed, then the mind has to follow suit. So practising daily relaxation should be a delightful priority.

There are a number of ways to induce relaxation which are easy to learn and can be practised alone.

The 7/11 method

- Settle yourself comfortably in a place where you won't be disturbed, ensuring your clothes are loose.
- Sit with your hands side by side in your lap or lie with your arms by your side, and your legs uncrossed.
- Close your eyes.
- Concentrate on becoming aware of your feet on the floor, of your arms and legs, wherever they are resting, and your head against the cushion, pillow or chair back.
- Keep your shoulders down and take in, through your nose, as deep a breath as you can manage. The air is pulled down to the bottom of your lungs when you breathe in deeply and this causes your stomach to inflate like a balloon. Count to seven as you breathe in. You will know you are breathing correctly when you feel your stomach rising as you place your hand gently across your stomach.
- Breathe out slowly, through your nose, making your out-breath last longer than your in-breath, allowing your stomach to deflate again. Count to eleven as you breathe out.

- Repeat these in-breaths and out-breaths ten or twenty times. If you can't breathe out for so long, try holding your breath as you finish the count to eleven or else try breathing in slowly to the count of three, and then out, slowly, to the count of five.

Make sure you breathe in and out through your nose and keep your mouth closed. This warms and filters the air inhaled and prevents you from losing too much carbon dioxide when you exhale. Carbon dioxide helps cells in the body use the oxygen that you breathe in. Concentrate on the counting and, if your mind wanders off, just gently bring your attention back and feel the welcome sense of calm flow in as you let over-busy thoughts go. Try to focus on fully inflating your lungs, seeing the rising of your stomach and not your shoulders. The most important thing is that the out-breaths last longer than your in-breaths. The 7/11 technique is excellent for calming yourself down instantly, if you need to, because you can do it 'on the go' and no one will know.

Clenched fist

This method is derived from yoga and is based on the principle that if a muscle or set of muscles is first tightly contracted and then relaxed, the relaxation effect is greatly enhanced. However, it is not advised if you have painful arthritis in the hand joints.

- Make your hands into the tightest fists possible, concentrating on noticing the whiteness of knuckles, the feeling of nails against your palms, the pressure of thumb against forefingers, the rigidity of wrists and elbows.
- Once all your attention is focused on this tension, allow the fingers and hands slowly to unwind and concentrate on the enjoyable sensations as your muscles relax. Focus

on the pleasant tingling sensation spreading through your fingers, up your arms and throughout your body causing tension to melt away.

- You can also do a whole-body version of this, beginning with your feet, moving up to your calves, knees, thighs, abdominal muscles and so on. You start by tensing each for a count of ten and then relaxing them, savouring the sensation.

Stand strong

At the heart of independence is the ability to make decisions for oneself. It is a core principle and implies autonomy over our own lives, which is the norm for most adults. Challenges in terms of health and mobility can get in the way of a person's desire to remain independent, generating inner tension and external conflict with those around us, who may try and limit the scope of our independence – often citing safety concerns.

It is important to ask ourselves periodically if our independence is under threat because other people are making decisions on our behalf without consultation, perhaps involving key issues such as where we should live and the level of support and practical assistance we need to stay in the community. Social and care services often decide such matters on behalf of older people and, along with severely risk-averse children of older adults, may wrap the older person in cotton wool, attempting to prevent every domestic mishap. The risk here is that our natural abilities and life skills become so underestimated that we can become deskilled in the most crucial aspects of daily living.

I think older people in general need to be a lot less timid in speaking up about the type of support systems they need, and that they can play a valuable role in advocating for the needs of others. I suggest older people become passionate, enthusiastic and even opinionated, to avoid a damaging passivity and timidity and to protect their independence. They should reinforce the stance that, even if they need support, they are still in charge of the process. The smart older person will renegotiate relationships with adult children, maintaining assertiveness.

Assuming mental capacity

Expectations of financial support from adult children may need to be severely modified in the light of costly private home care or other expenses. Older people frequently come under repeated pressure from adult children to bail them out financially, or to liquidate their assets by giving the younger generation a living legacy. This may not always be inappropriate, as generous parents may have long had an ambition to help their offspring achieve financial milestones partially or in full, but the timing of this is crucial if the older parent is to retain financial independence. Older people can bolster their decision-making ability by assuming ownership of most, if not all, of their healthcare and financial decisions (while they can) but should be willing to receive as much information as possible from others, to allow them to make healthy and balanced life choices. Personal decision-making should be promoted, should not be rushed or forced and should cover as many minor, everyday decisions as possible, such as meal and clothing choices or social activities, to prove competency and agency in bigger choices, such as care or home adaptations.

I would advise the loved ones or helpers of older people that, if assistance with certain tasks is needed, it should be assumed that the person requires only *some* or *partial* assistance with the task in question, rather than for it to be taken over entirely. If independence is assumed to be possible, and recoverable even if temporarily impaired by illness, then the ultimate goal of the vast majority of older people to live independently in their own homes, without being be a burden, will be realised.

A wonderful legacy

A rich legacy is available to us when we gracefully accept the wisdom, maturity and mellowing that goes with old age. The example we set for others, by demonstrating a level of acceptance of loss and grief, and of the hard blows and wounds that life has landed on us, is powerful. All the scars and hurts of the older generation contain lessons not only to be carried but also to be passed along. For the young who may be buffeted by impulses and expectations, the gratification of which is hard or impossible to delay, it is salutary to see that the hard edges of a personality can soften over time. Equally instructive is the fact that hot tempers can cool, rashness can be tempered by patience and the general foolishness of youth can be replaced with the wisdom of the years. The fact of the matter is that our greatest legacy is not the material goods we leave behind, which inevitably fade, but the example we give by demonstrating resilience and our ability to self-transcend, whilst remaining open to change yet without abandoning our principles and traditions.

With less time ahead, and even with the near proximity of the ending of the natural human lifespan, the potential for the enjoyment of life to accelerate exists. Whilst passion may not be the first emotion or state of being one associates with our later years, those who tamely follow trends out of fear, at any age, are actually the ones who are just going through the motions and who risk missing out. Older people, by contrast, can no longer make concessions on life's purpose and potential – it is now that they must venture out to seek untouched frontiers in the form of a skill they have not yet learned, a place they have never been, or a relationship they have not nurtured. Leveraging our time wisely is the ultimate stance to take in old age.

Looking at life through a lens of curiosity is a lot more fulfilling than wallowing in regrets of lost hopes and dreams, particularly if we realise that our opinions and actions still matter and that, as long as we are alive, we still have time to fulfil goals and dreams. Squeezing the last drops out of life is about writing our own history, even if we're on the last chapter and we're hoping for a bit more time to add a sequel or pen a new edition.

Arguably the most valuable human commodity and the hardest to harness in older age is energy. Yet curiosity, the human desire to know exactly what's around the next corner, is a great energy enhancer – as long as we don't forget to live in the present moment.

To savour every day of life as an older person there needs to be awareness of the myths that may be peddled about old age and what activities and behaviours others may deem to be appropriate. We can still be radical, proactive, full of opinions and committed to life in our twilight years. Our passion for family in the broadest sense, our interest in community and our personal ethos and belief systems are all about safeguarding and improving the society we are passing on to the next generation. Older people can influence, shape and contribute to every endeavour much more than they realise. Their collective voice will get a hearing – and the young will remove their headphones and listen.

PART III
Dealing effectively with mental distress: professional help

'The good physician treats the disease, but the great physician treats the person who has the disease.'

Sir William Osler

While it is by no means a given that older people will need psychological help at some point in their lives, it is also true that, because of the way that society is configured, older age can be a particularly testing time for many, and professional help may need to be called upon at some time. So it is important to ensure that the best and most appropriate help is given, especially as older age now encompasses a great many years, meaning that needs will vary enormously within that span.

Ethics in health care of older people

Professional ethics are important at any age but particularly so in relation to older people, if they are no longer able to take decisions for themselves and may be more easily swayed by the concerns or beliefs of younger relatives.

Health professionals who work with older people continually deal with ethical issues relating to the concerns of their clients but also to the concerns of those involved in their clients' care. In a normal course of events (and for many older people, too, of course) medical and psychotherapeutic encounters run as follows: the patient or client notices a problem and seeks help; therapeutic options are suggested and explanations and reassurances are given, which the patient/client is free to accept or not.

We health professionals have a duty, however, to ensure that consent or refusal to follow an intervention is fully informed. While a decision to refuse help should always be respected as long as the person is not endangering themselves or anyone else, in practice, if sufficient time is given for the person to explain why they have come to their decision and for the practitioner to explain why they think a different decision would be in their better interests, an initially reluctant individual may change their mind and be glad that they did so. In my mind, to deny time and space to discuss and weigh and reflect upon a given course of action is as bad as coercing a person into having a treatment or therapy.

Conversely, it is important to remember that many older people feel safer accepting the wisdom and judgement of a health professional. They may come from a generation whose values included trust and automatic respect for doctors, and although this may come as a surprise to many a clinician or therapist accustomed to dealing with resistance, easy compliance should never be used as a pretext for short circuiting discussion or dialogue.

When people have dementia, however, the course of events may be very different. They may not notice any difficulty nor do they seek help. If they are persuaded to attend for assessment, they may, unfortunately, be unable to understand or remember the diagnosis that is given, the therapeutic options offered or the implications of accepting or declining a given intervention. This lack of mental capacity or decision-making ability raises questions about the role of a proxy decision-maker – i.e. whether someone else, acting on their behalf, should make decisions for them.

Whose needs?

Central to an ethical approach to decision-making is the premise that older adults retain the ability to give and withhold consent until there is evidence to the contrary. We have already looked at the importance of autonomy and control and this should never lightly be cast aside. When the point is reached when autonomy does have to be set aside, however, professionals have a duty to ensure that the substitute decision-maker is acting in the best interests of the adult with dementia, rather for their own good or peace of mind.

It is also important to try and establish whose agenda is centre stage. Is the practitioner being asked to 'fix' the older client to better help whoever referred them meet their own needs? Does a daughter's desire for her mother to be less needy and dependent stem, for instance, from her *own* desire for her mother to demand less of her time? Does a son's desire for a parent to be labelled with a diagnosis of mental illness emanate from a desire to take over control of his parent's assets to alleviate his own financial problems? Or is there an agenda to avoid that middle-of-the-night phone call from a distressed, help-seeking father or mother by placing a parent prematurely in institutional care?

Another very important pitfall to look out for is that, even where there is a loving and caring family relationship, clinicians or therapists can find themselves compromised by the all-too-human tendency to identify with family members closest to their own age, and thus sympathise with their agenda and with what they want. Thus it can be easy sometimes to get sucked into supporting what the younger people believe will make their own lives easier. The skilled therapist will find ways to ensure that everyone's needs are fully understood and met, although it may take a lot of patient engagement in listening to and exploring the fears of each party before a way forward to accommodate everyone's best interest can be crafted. This may be based, for example, around the need for a secure and safe environment where the older person can have certain needs met and critical supports attended to without their independence being unnecessarily eroded.

Persuading an older person to accept a course of action which family members are suggesting can often be easily justified – to accept home help or carer support, for example, in the case of a person who is struggling to live independently. The latter may struggle with any number of misconceptions, such as this being the beginning of the slippery slope, or react purely reflexively with a negative response, and all that may be required in these situations is a little extra time to explain patiently and reassure. On the other hand, the reason that an older person may decline to accept support could be for the sake of preserving the daily living skills and overall independence they still have, even when this brings safety concerns and risk. This 'quality of life' aspect is important to take into account – life, after all, is not risk free for any age group and surely acknowledgement of personal autonomy includes choosing to live with an acceptable level of risk.

Four pillars of ethical practice

Ethical principles are often based on the so-called four pillars of good ethical practice, autonomy being just one of them. The principle of *justice* holds that people deserve access to the best care and treatment depending on need, not chronological age. But what if the treatment a person wants is too invasive or undignified, such as where care interventions escalate to include measures such as bladder catheterisation, nasogastric feeding or artificial ventilation, even though the overall prognosis is very poor? Whilst most people will want everything done to stay alive during any illness, if the person is already debilitated and has a poor quality of life, then overly aggressive treatment may be inappropriate to their individual circumstances. The clearest example may be performing cardio-pulmonary resuscitation (CPR) in people who are terminally ill or in cases of advanced dementia. The procedure has a low chance of success and care interventions resulting from it may escalate, thus over-medicalising the care of people who are dying, denying them dignity and comfort.

In such cases, we have to be guided by the principles of *beneficence* (doing good) and *non-maleficence* (avoiding harm). Again the example of CPR serves to highlight how doctors are not obliged to and should not offer overly invasive interventions that are unlikely to be of benefit (avoiding harm) and could even increase suffering – this could even apply to chemotherapy, where side effects are severe and benefits gained in late-stage illness marginal.

The principle of beneficence concerns action that promotes the well-being of others, namely patients and their families, but may involve a judgement call by the professional as to what treatment option is appropriate and proportionate to the problem. For instance, older people's access to psychotherapy is often poor, not just because of under-resourcing and prioritising in favour of younger people, but also because of professional ignorance of its potential benefit. There is an onus on health professionals who come in contact with distressed older people, therefore, to recommend therapy whenever it is deemed appropriate, to help dispel ignorance and misconceptions about its lack of efficacy and advocate for its availability based on the evidence of effectiveness. We will be looking in detail later at what good, brief psychotherapy can help achieve.

Sometimes good ethical practice in therapy is about acknowledging the conflict between ethical goals – finding the balance between, for example, urging an intervention which we perceive as helpful whilst respecting the right of individuals to direct their own lives as far as is possible. Arriving at good ethically based decisions may ultimately depend on the quality of the information that is available. If a decision is vexed and the decision-makers perplexed, going the extra mile to obtain additional information or the perspectives of others may reveal the right way forward. If there is impaired mental capacity, we can at least attempt to act in accordance with what a person might have wished by finding out as much as possible about their life choices and preferences *before* capacity was lost. (It is best, of course, if this can be found out from the individuals themselves, while they still have their cognitive abilities.)

Depression in later life

The major mental health difficulty that affects older people is depression. As I have already indicated, there can be confusion among professionals about its nature. Such confusion can lead us to neglect what is a serious condition that may require urgent treatment (depression may manifest as a severe illness in up to 3 per cent of over-65s) or, at the other end of the spectrum, to overreact to a normal emotional state (sadness or difficulty in adjusting to changed circumstances). The distinction between the two is critical as it has enormous implications for long-term mental and physical well-being and even longevity.

Clinical or major depression should be called out for what it is – an abnormal emotional state or an illness that affects thinking, emotions, perception and behaviour in pervasive and chronic ways. There may not be an immediately apparent triggering event but some older people will report a greater number of health events or a top-tier life stressor in the months and weeks before it manifests itself. Often people's lives may 'on paper' seem totally fine, even enviable, and yet they still feel horrible.

We know that depression in older people can lead to increased risk of cardiac disease and overall mortality from other conditions, not to mention being associated with an increased risk of suicide in older white men. Stigma and shame particularly may prevent older people from seeking professional help. They may often be deeply embarrassed about acknowledging emotional distress to themselves, never mind an outsider, perceiving this as a sign of personal weakness. Fortunately, attitudes are changing and the 'baby boomer' generation is, in general, more emotionally literate and has higher expectations of later years than the preceding generation of retirees.

Depression colours all aspects of life, making everything seem less enjoyable and not worth the effort. It can sap energy, vitality and the ability to experience pleasure, joy, anticipation, satisfaction, connection or meaning in life. Other symptoms include difficulties with sleep and appetite and some bodily functions seem to operate on a slower gear. Movement may be slower, while concentration and memory may be frustratingly ponderous and impaired. Perception of pain in any region of the body from pre-existing medical conditions may be intensified and, if weight loss accompanies this, a flurry of medical investigations can ensue if a doctor is consulted for advice. The general lethargy and debility associated with depression can mimic many physical illnesses, but it is often only when tests return negative or results are inconclusive that the possibility of a psychological underpinning to a myriad of non-specific symptoms gets considered.

The diagnosis of depression in an older population may be confounded, as we have seen, by more atypical or unusual features, while the classic features such as emotional sadness may be completely absent – or are actively denied, for aforementioned reasons. Even if some older people with depression do display typical features such as loss of pleasure and interest in things or tiredness, others inadvertently challenge the diagnostic skills of clinicians by displaying less recognisable features of low mood. These can include a change in behaviour – hostility or agitation, for example, or an increased consumption of alcohol or, indeed, any new or out of character conduct which is dysfunctional or out of keeping with their usual personality. I recall patients in nursing homes often perplexing staff by starting to throw themselves on the floor – a behaviour that can frequently be accounted for by the presence of undiagnosed depression. This behaviour may be completely uncharacteristic of the person and can reflect the stripping away of our mature defences as we become more and more depressed. Being unable to self-appraise this alien inner emotional state, the depressed older person may find no other way to communicate their distress to others than by engaging in behaviour that can seem almost like an adult equivalent of a tantrum.

Depression is the commonest mental health difficulty in older people, with an estimated 10–15 per cent of those living in the community suffering from it. We must be clear, however, that there is no evidence that the incidence or prevalence of depression increases with advancing age. The rates do increase, though, within medical settings. As many as 10 per cent of older adults admitted to general hospitals exhibit major depression.[1] Rates of significant depression in nursing homes are worryingly high, with depressive symptoms detectable in up to 35 per cent of residents. The reasons for this are complex; it may be tempting to blame a lack of privacy in nursing homes or poor-quality care or routines that are under-stimulating for residents, but it has to be borne in mind that the people who need nursing-home care may be particularly frail and already struggling with medical and cognitive issues such as dementia which, in themselves, are highly associated with depression.

Suicidal thinking in older people should always be taken seriously in any care setting, as suicide is relatively common among older adults, especially among those who have physical health problems. Whereas younger people in distress may 'cry for help' without being clinically depressed, non-lethal self-harming behaviour in old age is very rare and implies at least moderately significant depression.

Anxiety in later life

Late-life anxiety is a common problem across all cultures and, as a symptom, can be an indirect expression of need for help in maintaining activities of daily living, when abilities are

---

1   David Ames et al., *Guide to the Psychiatry of Old Age*, Cambridge: Cambridge University Press, 2010, p. 75.

becoming more compromised. Anxiety can also be associated with various physical symptoms, such as the breathlessness that arises from lung disease or heart failure, but may also stem from fear of falling and even from having to be away from where one feels safe. Anxiety that is unwittingly minimised or ignored by clinicians can become a vicious circle, leading older people to avoid putting themselves in situations that cause them anxiety, potentially creating social isolation, which in turn leads to feelings of loneliness and depression, consequently raising anxiety levels even further.

There is an old saying that later life is the most refreshing of life's stages, where we care less and dare more. While younger people get stressed even thinking about stress, many older people can more easily be helped to see panicky anxiety for what it is – namely, a good aerobic workout, caused by rapid heartbeat with or without palpitations, and not the sign of a heart attack! Or else anxiety can be viewed as a useful (if not an over-zealous) security guard within one's brain to warn of impending danger or threats. There is some truth in the observation that many anxiety disorders, such as obsessive compulsive disorder and generalised anxiety disorder, rarely make an appearance as a new disorder in old age. This is even true of post-traumatic stress disorder (PTSD), perhaps to do with reduced mobility leading to less exposure to triggers such as assault or mugging, although this is terrifying when it does happen. Also, older-age experiences around having a stroke or delirium can be perceived as highly traumatic. However, overall, PTSD occurrence is much rarer in later life than in younger populations.

Similarly, pre-existing conditions such as social anxiety, panic disorder or generalised anxiety disorders tend to be less severe as we advance in years and can, in effect, burn themselves out with the passage of time. Phobia (in which severe anxiety arises in response to situations which are not dangerous) seems to be the most common anxiety disorder in older populations, affecting 3–6 per cent of older people – especially agoraphobia, a fear of uncontrollable outside situations, often involving crowds of people and situations which are difficult to escape from. The onset is usually later than for other phobias, such as fear of spiders, flying or heights, and can occur after a distressing event while out alone (for instance, being mugged), causing the person to become housebound.

Yet again, the black cloud of depression seems to dominate and even envelop the psychological landscape, as most of the anxiety that arises *de novo* in later life is in fact secondary to major depression. Some clinicians would even go so far as to suggest that *any* new onset anxiety in older age should suggest a depressive disorder. It is also important to be aware that excessive worry and anxiety symptoms are commonly found in people with dementia. This may be seen as an understandable reaction to emerging cognitive deficits, but the heightened anxiety can itself increase struggles with daily recall, as it can literally 'knock out' memory and artificially depress cognitive performance.

We know that disproportionate and persistent activation of the stress-sensitive areas of the brain produces anxiety, panic attacks and even depression (which is a state of excessive arousal, not under-arousal of the brain, as we might have thought). Excess worry has the effect of disrupting the balance of sleep, resulting in longer periods of intense dream sleep (known as rapid eye movement, or REM, sleep because of the rapid eye movements that occur under the closed eyelids while dreaming), and reduced periods of recuperative slow-wave sleep. Dream sleep uses up a lot of energy and the excess which occurs in anxiety/depression prompts early morning wakening in a state of exhaustion, a state which persists during the first half of the day. It is no surprise, therefore, that people who experience depression have low levels of energy and concentration in the mornings.

Additionally, persistently elevated stress hormone levels, such as increased concentrations of cortisol, have the effect of killing off cells in the brain's seat of memory (the hippocampus). This partially explains why deficits in learning and memory can accompany persistent stress in older people and why depression and increased stress are risk factors for dementia in older people. High levels of cortisol may damage the body's immune system, putting a person who is stressed at greater risk of infection. Chronic stress is therefore the enemy of health in the mind and in the body and it is absolutely crucial to lower it.

'Depression and increased stress are risk factors for dementia in older people.'

In the successful treatment of depression in older people, both psychological and drug approaches can play their part, according to individual circumstances. It is now appreciated, however, that, in mild-to-moderate depression, psychotherapy has an efficacy equivalent to antidepressants and the same benefits as psychological treatment in a younger population.

Declining memory and late-life dementia

There is a lot of public awareness, and fear, about Alzheimer's disease but there is little public knowledge, in my experience, of the normal age-associated changes in memory and cognitive ability and the fact that these changes in themselves do not progress to dementia. As mentioned in Part II of this book, it is quite normal not to recall a name of a semi-acquaintance or to struggle to remember the name of a famous actor or to have difficulty retrieving a word or two. Equally, going upstairs and not remembering why happens to us all and does not generally indicate a significant problem with memory.

There is also little awareness of how we may be putting our brains at risk. Alcohol is a well-known killer of liver cells but it can be a potent killer of brain cells too. There are numerous reasons to moderate one's alcohol intake as we get older; it is a depressant that negatively affects mood, and it damages cells in three key brain regions, namely the frontal lobe (the part of the brain governing social and emotional regulation/decision-making/abstract thinking and judgement), the hippocampus (memory centre of the brain) and the cerebellum (governing co-ordinated movement and balance). By realising our ability to influence our brain health positively by reducing dangerous levels of alcohol, we can develop a sense of autonomy and mastery over this aspect of our lives.

Most older adults retain the cognitive capability to live a full and enriched life but a minority of older people do develop dementia and cognitive problems in later years. Before saying more, a few definitions would seem appropriate. Dementia is an acquired impairment of intellect, memory and personality which is progressive – although sometimes reversible in a small number of cases. Alzheimer's disease is the top cause of dementia, not a separate and more severe illness, as is often thought. Other common causes of dementia include vascular or mini-stroke-related issues, essentially where there is a gradual impairment of blood supply to the brain, leading to brain-cell death and the consequent emergence of symptoms.

A variety of symptoms

There is a common misperception that cognitive decline is an inevitable part of ageing and it is important to remember that any such decline can be due to many causes and presentations can vary widely. In mild cognitive impairment, the memory or cognitive issues are not sufficient to compromise the person's day-to-day functioning and not everyone with this milder form of difficulty will progress to dementia.

Symptoms of dementia include forgetfulness, namely difficulty in taking in and retaining information or repeating questions as short-term memory declines and information seems to 'stick' less well. Difficulty with language and finding words or naming objects is common and comprehension may also be affected. Disorientation of time is a common early symptom; difficulty in manipulating objects such as smartphones or remote controls requiring fine motor movements may appear later. If a person has visuospatial problems (difficulty locating objects in space or navigating one's way around) driving ability may be affected, although this is not inevitable and many people with dementia continue to drive safely at least in the early stages of the condition.

Most of us can compensate for occasional memory lapses but it is when higher order abilities such as decision-making, planning and exercising judgement get affected that life may become very challenging, and that is often what brings people to medical attention. Changes in personality can be a core feature of early onset and certain other types of dementias but more subtle personality difficulties, such as a reduction in empathy or disinhibition, can be common in other dementia subtypes.

Risk factors

Age is the single biggest risk factor for dementia, virtually irrespective of the cause. The prevalence of Alzheimer's disease doubles every four and a half years after the age of 65, peaking at a 50–60 per cent prevalence by one's mid nineties. Less than one per cent of all Alzheimer's disease is familial and, while the overall risk of Alzheimer's is greater in women, men may be more susceptible to vascular dementia. Other general risk factors include head injury, low level of formal education, alcohol excess and nutritional deficiencies. The diagnosis of dementia requires a thorough clinical assessment and this may be supplemented by other tests such as brain scanning or detailed memory tests (neuropsychological assessment) undertaken by a specially trained psychologist. Occasionally, potentially reversible causes of dementia are diagnosed, such as an underactive thyroid gland or vitamin B12 deficiency. It is, of course, gratifying for a clinician to pick up on and treat such cases.

Management priorities

Management of dementia should involve many professionals from the outset. Multidisciplinary assessment is essential for assessing how well a person can function and evaluating mental and physical health issues and safety concerns. There should be adequate time allowed for coping with whatever may arise from the sharing of this very difficult diagnosis and its implications. Many people fear the worst and imagine rapid decline and loss of independence, yet, in reality, very little may change in terms of lifestyle for quite a while and sometimes for long periods – some cases are only very slowly progressive and thus the condition may have a lengthy and protracted course. Even after a diagnosis of Alzheimer's disease is confirmed, it may be very hard for clinicians to predict the trajectory of progression that may follow, as there is so much variation in how this illness may unfold. Vascular dementia, for instance, may have a lengthy plateau phase with little decline initially and often it is only when an acute infection or other medical event occurs on top of the memory disorder that a stepwise decline may be seen.

'Some cases of dementia are only very slowly progressive and thus the condition may have a lengthy and protracted course.'

The benefits of finding out

Understandably, people may resist coming for an initial discussion of their problems with their trusted family doctor, let alone an assessment. Difficult as it may be, no one should ever be deterred from attending a memory clinic or other service skilled in the assessment of cognitive complaints and memory disorders. It is not true that 'nothing can be done' about dementia, as some people may try to tell you. Attending at an early stage allows the chance of delaying the progression of dementia through treatment. However, just as importantly, sometimes severe depression masquerades as dementia (so-called pseudodementia) and people can be reassured and sent on a completely different treatment pathway. Others may attend fearing the worst, convinced that they are no longer safe to drive, but come away with a 'less severe' diagnosis, such as mild cognitive impairment or age-related memory impairment, and are reassured that they remain safe and competent in their driving ability.

What is without doubt is that burying one's head in the sand and ignoring memory complaints is likely to fuel depression and anxiety, making the memory problem worse. People can get into a pessimistic and negative spiral of self-criticism, excessively focusing on everyday mistakes and catastrophising their causes and consequences. Having a 'business-like' approach to checking out memory is the best way ultimately to alleviate anxiety, understand normal age-related changes and contextualise abnormal changes.

Even when the diagnosis is indeed dementia, individuals may vary enormously in terms of what they wish to be told about their diagnosis, and both family and professionals need to be sensitive to this. Very often family members ask that their loved ones be protected from information as the diagnosis of dementia is so highly stigmatised and feared, yet knowledge ultimately is power while people still have mental capacity to make key life decisions, settle financial affairs and decide lifestyle priorities, which might include travel.

Professionals cannot offer false reassurance about the curability of the condition but can indeed give honest and straightforward advice about how the condition may respond to treatment. A therapeutic approach may vary from medication to elevate the levels of acetylcholine, a key neurotransmitter involved in memory, to signposting services and supports that can make a significant difference to quality of life. If the dementia is at a more advanced stage at diagnosis, the person may have little insight into the condition and it is reasonable not to batter down their defences with hard information, instead tailoring information to their level of understanding.

Drug treatments for psychological ill-health

In Ireland and the UK, only GPs and psychiatrists can prescribe psychotropic medication (drugs that affect mental state). Psychiatrists are doctors who specialise in the assessment, diagnosis and treatment of many forms of mental illness, including those found exclusively in an older population. Ideally, psychotropic medications in older people should be given only as part of a broad treatment plan, addressing the complexity of overall need. It stands to reason, for instance, that problems such as loneliness and isolation are unlikely to be helped by medication.

When there doesn't seem to be many therapeutic options on offer, doctors may all too easily succumb to the prescribing reflex in a genuine desire to help. (Many older people may be uncomplaining about taking many medications, as they may have become accustomed to taking a wide variety of them for all sorts of conditions and complaints, while in other cases psychiatrists will struggle to convince patients to take a single medication as part of a treatment plan.) However, inappropriate prescriptions of hypnotics, anti-anxiety drugs and antidepressants may lead to potentially serious side effects, putting the patient at risk of daytime sedation, falls and cognitive and memory impairment.

The potential for side effects is greater in older people because drugs may not be metabolised as rapidly in the ageing body, leading to increased levels within the bloodstream. Additionally, we know that many psychotropic medications are not immediately broken down in an older person, and bind to fat stores within the older body (the proportion of body fat sadly increasing for most us as we get older). This means that the drugs continue to be slowly released, on top of the regular daily dose that is being ingested, leading to a double-dosing effect. It is thus important that doctors prescribe substantially lower doses of most drugs for most conditions in older people.

The main priority for older patients thus may be to ensure that they are taking the 'right' medication or fewer of them as, when medications for a variety of conditions are given in combination, there is a greater potential for side effects and drug-to-drug interactions. This can cause reluctance among some practitioners to prescribe *at all* for mental health difficulties in an older population. This may be no bad thing, as it encourages clinicians to look at other potential solutions to psychological issues and non-drug options for treating depression and anxiety. On the other hand, there is a risk that depression, particularly, can quickly worsen or become a life-threatening health problem, or that everyday distress may not be adequately alleviated. The balance thus must be struck between the risks of under-treating or not treating, which may be greater than the risks associated with medications.

Drugs to treat psychiatric disorders are now among the most widely prescribed forms of medication. In the US, for example, antidepressants are second only to cholesterol-lowering agents in prescription volume. I believe that the act of prescribing must always be to alleviate specific aspects of a condition, with an eye to safety and avoiding causing more harm than good. Coming to a decision about this is not helped by the fact that most research studies on the use and safety of drugs is conducted on younger groups of people, so the benefits and risks associated with individual medications may differ in an older population of patients. As explained, as we age, our body's ability to break down drugs is significantly reduced, resulting in the build-up of doses causing more rapid therapeutic effects, but also adverse effects, at lower than expected doses.

Traditionally, medications used to treat serious mental illness have been divided into four categories:

- Antipsychotic drugs or 'neuroleptics', used to treat psychosis
- Antidepressant medications, used to treat depression
- Antimanic or mood-stabilising drugs, used to treat bipolar mood disorder (episodic extreme high and low moods)
- Anti-anxiety or anxiolytic drugs, used to treat anxious states and sometimes insomnia.

These distinctions are less clear-cut in practice, as medications licensed for one condition can and often are used in other disorders too – for example, many antidepressants are prescribed for anxiety disorders. Drugs from all four categories may be used to treat problematic symptoms such as insomnia, impulse control or behavioural disturbance in dementia. Other medicines that would not primarily be classified as psychotropic drugs may also be prescribed to treat a range of psychological symptoms, such as beta blockers for anxiety or antihistamines for insomnia.

Older people and medicines – a special population

Older people, as I have said, will require lower doses of medication compared to younger adults, and clinicians and patients alike should also be aware of the potential for drug-to-drug interactions. The best maxim for prescribing in an older age group is to 'start low and go slow'. Some medicines can literally be different compounds at different doses, and the side effects that appear at high doses may be totally absent when the dose is reduced. Older people over the age of 70 should, in general, initially receive about one-half to one-third of the usual adult dose of any medicine, with the dose being raised gradually and in small amounts until a clinical benefit appears. (Any unacceptable adverse effects that occur will limit the dose escalation or titration, of course.) Even much smaller doses of medication (sometimes as little as one-tenth of a standard adult dose) may be effective in some older people.

It may end up that some older people do require the usual adult doses of medicines, whilst others respond to much lower levels. Not every doctor will be aware of this need to tailor doses of medication to each person.

'Much smaller doses of medication (sometimes as little as one-tenth of a standard adult dose) may be effective in some older people.'

The major side effects and concerns when exposing older people to psychotropic drugs include low blood pressure, cardiac rhythm disturbances and cognitive disturbances, including sedation and/or confusion. Rarer side effects, but equally concerning, are imbalances in blood biochemistry, due to reduced sodium levels or deteriorating kidney or liver function. It is vital, therefore, that both prescriber and patient keep an eye on things, with the patient knowing what problems to be alert to and report.

Older people tend to rely less than younger people on the internet for sources of information on medicines, although this is gradually changing. So it is important that people stay 'on top' of the psychotropic medications they are prescribed, just as I suggested in Part I for other medications.

Questions that older people can and should put to their doctors and pharmacists include:

- What is my medication for?
- Is it safe to drive whilst taking this treatment?
- What side effects are to be expected and what should I do if this occurs?
- How long do I need to take this treatment for?
- What should I do if I forget to take a dose?
- Are there any tests or monitoring required whilst taking this medicine?
- Is this medication safe to take with my other tablets?

Keeping a personal record of prescribed medication is very helpful (and should include medicines that have been stopped or substances that the person is allergic to). As mentioned before, memory aids such as a daily or weekly pill box may provide a convenient means of organising medication, especially if the patient has memory impairment and forgets to take them. The only drawback with this method of pre-packing and pre-arranging medicines is that the user becomes less familiar with and less inquisitive about their medication, as their only responsibility is obediently to ingest the tablets from each compartment of the blister pack.

A 'skills as well as pills' approach

Medication may, for people with severe symptoms of mental illness, do a lot of heavy lifting in terms of enabling people to engage with other therapies. When the anxiety or the depression symptoms are lowered, for instance, people can have more capacity to address difficult circumstances in their life or see what they need to do differently. Psychotropic medication that is prescribed indefinitely, however, risks sending a message that only chemical substances can 'fix' a person's difficulties, making innate resources and problem-solving skills seem irrelevant. I believe this disrespects the resilience and innate coping abilities of individuals who choose to use medication as a therapeutic instrument for a period of time and then may choose to wean themselves off it, when such intervention is no longer necessary.

However, it is my clinical experience that the decision to withdraw, albeit gradually, any psychotropic drug is fraught with danger. It is often difficult to gauge whether or not one should 'rock the boat' when a person appears to have recovered from an acute episode of illness, especially if treatment appears to be well tolerated. Whilst instinctively most prescribers will want to taper down medication, to do so too soon can invite discontinuation or withdrawal symptoms, which may be hard to distinguish from full-blown relapse.

In general, after a first episode of acute illness, most doctors will advise maintenance treatment for at least six to nine months after full recovery, assuming the medication has had a part to play in the improvement. Older people, however, may be at a higher risk of relapse (within six months after recovery) and recurrence (after six months of recovery) than younger people. For a second episode, maintenance treatment may be advised for eighteen months, and for a third or further episodes treatment may be continued for much longer. The question is, for how long? In reality it is a case-by-case decision.

Withdrawal symptoms may depend on the type of psychotropic agent in question – hypnotics or sleeping tablets have withdrawal symptoms that most prominently include rebound wakefulness, whereas antidepressant withdrawal symptoms may include dizziness, nausea, tingling in muscles, anxiety and dip in mood. This may be very hard to distinguish from the original condition for which the drug was prescribed but, in general, the body adapts to the absence of the medication by itself and such symptoms are self-limiting (generally peaking at two days after the last dose, beginning to subside within five days and disappearing completely within weeks of cessation). If re-emerging symptoms persist for longer than a few weeks, then a return of the original condition should be suspected. However, it is now recognised that discontinuation effects from antidepressants can sometimes persist for weeks and even months, although thankfully this is not common.

Stopping mood stabilisers or antipsychotics abruptly may be associated with insomnia, anxiety, agitation, severe mood changes and even a return of psychotic symptoms, but that is not to say gradual cessation of such medication cannot be attempted – it just needs to be done over a timeframe of weeks or months depending on the duration of prior treatment.

The longer a person stays on medication, as a rule, the harder it is to discontinue it. We do not yet know the long-term effects on brain biochemistry of any psychotropic agent but, for people who have been exposed for decades, it may be nearly impossible to stop certain drugs. I have frequently witnessed terrible scenarios of severe withdrawals from even very low doses of treatment and re-emergence of stress, depression or psychosis when doctors feel that treatment is no longer needed or fail to establish how long a person has been taking a given treatment. Such severe rebound effects can result in hospital admission in some circumstances.

The best strategy may be to taper down the dose cautiously, in close collaboration with a clinician with expertise in psychopharmacology or mental health medication. Alas, however, even this may be hit and miss, as it is not yet known, through scientific research, who can 'get away with' and benefit from coming off medication and who can't.

Older people taking certain treatments for physical health problems should also be aware that some are implicated in causing unintended adverse psychological effects:

- Painkillers such as opiates, steroids used in many inflammatory conditions, the heart medication digoxin and treatments used to counteract the symptoms of Parkinson's disease are well-known high-risk drugs for the causation of acute confusion and psychosis in older adults.
- Codeine-based painkillers (sold in many countries 'over the counter' and without a prescription) or older antidepressants (called tricyclic agents) have the tendency to worsen confusion by lowering the levels of acetylcholine in the brain.
- Anticholinergic drugs for conditions as diverse as diarrhoea, asthma and urinary incontinence can also deplete concentration of the neurotransmitter acetylcholine in the brain and affect learning and memory.
- Medications such as beta blockers that treat high blood pressure or heart conditions have been implicated in inducing depressive symptoms.
- Anticonvulsants, antimalarials, anti-ulcer medicines and high-dose statins to lower cholesterol have all been associated with the onset of depression.
- Benzodiazepines (the Valium family of minor tranquillisers) used to provide rapid relief of anxiety, along with the older tricyclic class of antidepressant drugs, are regularly linked with confusion in an older cohort of patients.

If such problems arise, a careful risk-benefit analysis in consultation with your prescriber, along with constant monitoring and review of any such side effects, is the best practice.

The case for more regular monitoring

Psychiatric medications that emerged during the 1990s, such as the serotonin-enhancing SSRI antidepressants and so-called atypical or newer generation antipsychotics, seem to be easier for older people, in particular, to tolerate. Biochemistry monitoring is recognised as prudent among all patients newly introduced to SSRIs to monitor potential emergence of low sodium in the blood; this can cause weakness, lethargy, nausea and impaired balance, to which older people are particularly susceptible. However, passing time has shown that even these ostensibly 'safer' medications need closer monitoring (with new guidelines published, rather amazingly, not until almost two decades after these medications were first introduced). Now, before starting treatment and every three to six months afterwards, a simple cardiac tracing or ECG to monitor cardiac rhythm is suggested.

Other antidepressants, such as the older tricyclic agents, are well known to cause a drop in blood pressure, and monitoring of this is important to help prevent falls. It is also important that prescribers are especially aware of the need for the deployment of small doses of these medications to avoid this.

It is now routine practice to monitor blood glucose and cholesterol levels in those taking antipsychotic medicines, because of the tendency of these drugs to induce weight gain. Even if it may be natural to accumulate a few extra pounds over the years it is not something to ignore, as this is a risk factor for stroke and heart disease. The potential adverse effects of antipsychotic medications for older people with dementia also include mini-strokes, aspiration pneumonia and dehydration due to sedation. Such risks have strongly encouraged doctors to stop using this category of medicines to deal with behavioural problems such as agitation or aggression in people with dementia and to try non-pharmacological interventions first.

To be fair, most psychotropic medications are probably no more dangerous to take on a long-term basis than many other drugs, such as anti-inflammatory medication, or blood pressure tablets, but the trick is to 'get away' with the lowest dose and give the medication time to act – often it might be weeks. Your doctor should arrange the appropriate checks, such as blood tests, cardiac tracings (ECGs), weight monitoring and blood pressure (if you feel dizzy on rising to stand), but it is good for you to stay aware of the need for these checks as well, and to keep liaising with your doctor to ensure that you are on the right dosage for your needs.

Medication does not offer a 'free lunch'. None is devoid of side effects and, particularly in the case of depression, may not always work well. Clinicians often observe that the severest form of depression, where there are many biological symptoms such as weight loss, early morning wakening and worsening of depression in the morning with tearfulness, tends to respond best to medical intervention with antidepressants, whereas medication may not alleviate less severe presentations. The same can sometimes be said for relapsing or chronic episodes of distress, which may not respond as well to drug treatment as in the first episode. Often combinations of medications are used to remit psychological symptoms and while this may be clinically successful, it directly adds to the risk of adverse effects and drug-to-drug interactions. Also, being asked to take so many medicines in combination may be repugnant to many patients, and also risks creating a misperception that their problems are especially grave.

There is both an art and a science to prescribing and monitoring mental health medication in older people, and advances in the area over the years have provided hope in conditions where none had existed, such as in Alzheimer's disease and other forms of dementia. It is important to remember that anti-dementia treatments fall under the general umbrella term of psychotropic medicines, and drugs that boost brain levels of the important neurotransmitter acetylcholine appear to stall for a time the inexorable decline seen in these common conditions. But we desperately need other agents that might reverse the disease process itself, which current therapy does not.

I think it important to stress that mental health prescribing should not be carried out in a therapeutic vacuum, where other interventions are simply bit players – if they get a look-in at all. Interventions that blend a broad-based, team-centred approach are far more likely to be taken up by service users and their families, and will avoid creating an over-dependency on one particular treatment model.

Psychological therapies for older people

While social interventions such as day centres, exercise groups and creative activities are frequently endorsed and even 'prescribed' for older people with a wide variety of mental health difficulties in later life, psychological treatment is, rather bizarrely, often underused by professionals working in this area. Older people as a group are definitely underrepresented amongst those accessing psychological therapies and services.

Yet we know that such therapies are as effective for older people as for those of working age or younger, even if the message hasn't got through to professionals. Data from the UK's National Health Service initiative for improving access to psychological therapies (IAPT) has shown that, once referred, a greater proportion of older adults (42 per cent) complete treatment than those of working age (37 per cent). In 2014–15, 56 per cent of over-65s showed reliable recovery after receiving psychological therapies, compared with 42 per cent of working age adults.[2]

So why isn't this positive message getting through? I would say that, on occasion, a sense of 'therapeutic nihilism' can infect social care and primary care professionals working alongside older clients, so that the level of severity of their problems may have to be especially serious and acute for referral for psychiatric care or psychological intervention to be recognised as warranted. Therapeutic pessimism and ageism may certainly account for the trend of very few people aged over 90 being referred for therapy, despite the multiple challenges in daily living being faced by this age group.

Some therapists also may lack confidence and experience in working with older patients or fear that models of therapy employed in younger age cohorts are inappropriate or overly optimistic for older people, despite there being absolutely no evidence for this. And mental health services may have rigid and entrenched professional boundaries when it comes to making limited resources available for older people, preferring to prioritise youth mental health or forensic services instead.

In some cases it is older people themselves who are unwilling to attend for therapy or can't see the point, assuming that psychotherapy is not relevant or is unlikely to be helpful in addressing difficulties, such as coping with poverty and isolation and the death of family and friends. It may even seem self-indulgent 'at my age'. Some may feel that the past simply cannot be changed, no matter how much it is talked about (I would agree – that is not the only way to do psychotherapy). Others may be intimidated by the

---

2   NHS Digital, *Psychological Therapies, Annual Report on the Use of IAPT Services – England 2016–17*, 2017, https://digital.nhs.uk/data-and-information/publications/statistical/psychological-therapies-annual-reports-on-the-use-of-iapt-services; accessed 15 April 2022.

(erroneous) belief that counselling means spending an hour on a couch, without knowing exactly what is expected of them. Older men, especially, may find it difficult to overcome the belief that emotions and feelings are not for discussion, and think they should project an outward air of 'coping', whether they are or not.

It is amazing how altruistic older people can be. Aware of how scarce and precious therapy time can be, they may even ask at the first session if the therapist would not prefer to devote their time to more deserving younger people instead. It is sad that older adults experiencing psychological difficulties do not feel entitled to receive the high-quality care and supports that their younger counterparts regularly receive and, indeed, expect. The message that they seem to internalise is that they should be grateful for having had a 'fair innings' up to now. I hope older people will begin to realise the extent of the valuable resources that they bring to the therapy encounter including, as we have seen, a wealth of knowledge, rich experience of life and wisdom to draw upon.

A broad range of services

Nowadays the old-age multidisciplinary team can include psychologists, occupational therapists, social workers, dieticians, dementia specialists, physiotherapists and community-based nursing staff. Valuable input can also be provided by psychotherapists and counsellors in primary care, health advocates, assisted decision-makers (advocates and family members appointed to act in the best interests of the person under legal arrangements) and by the essential services and supports offered by the voluntary sector. The Alzheimer Society, for instance, advocates not only for those who experience this condition, but also provides public information and education about dementia to de-stigmatise these and other illnesses that are still shrouded in fear, mythology and misconception.

Those working with older people require not just an interest, dedication and commitment to their concerns but also a deep understanding of family dynamics and the integrity to advocate for their clients when disputes or conflicting goals arise. Only a co-ordinated, flexible and person-centred approach will deliver healthcare needs to this section of society, and teams that offer physical or psychological care to older people should be wide-ranging, multidisciplinary and community-based. Therapeutic input for older people also often involves a degree of signposting to other relevant services that offer specific expertise not only to individuals affected but also to their caregivers and supporters.

Psychological therapies

Psychological therapies may most usually be offered by psychologists, counsellors and psychotherapists (the latter two are largely the same), either in primary or secondary care, or privately. In practice, though, it has to be ascertained first what, if any, psychological treatment is actually available to any one individual. Many community mental health teams allied to psychiatric services, for instance, may have little or no access to therapy, depending on factors such as the length of their waiting lists or resource issues in general. Equally, a particular therapist may have an allegiance to, or experience in, just one form of therapy and this may not entirely match the client's needs or be in keeping with recent treatment advances for specific disorders. I think it is extremely important that the therapy should fit the client and the client not be fitted to the therapy.

Whether standards models of therapy have much to offer such subgroups of older people remains an open question but nonetheless the following approaches have received academic attention:

Cognitive behavioural therapy (CBT) is based on the principle that how we think and how we act can influence our mood, rather than the other way round. Unhelpful beliefs and behaviours are identified and challenged cognitively (cognitive therapy) or behaviourally (through setting tasks). The therapy is quite rigidly structured (doesn't allow for wide flexibility and variation) and is focused on setting goals that modify thoughts, feelings and behaviours. Up to twenty weekly or fortnightly sessions may be required. (Proviso: The 'homework' associated with CBT is also not for the ambivalent, as it may require high levels of motivation and logical thinking to implement. This may not be appealing for many older people who see their self-efficacy fading by the day and who may feel that being talked out of their emotions is being entirely disrespectful of their state and their circumstances.)

Interpersonal therapy is based on the observation that difficulties with communication and within relationships have been associated with the onset and worsening of depressive symptoms. It focuses on issues such as grief or loss of a spouse, role transitions such as retirement, interpersonal disputes and distorted or unrealistic expectations of relationships, leading to perceived deficits in social support. This therapy is also quite rigidly structured and involves role playing, communication analysis, clarification of the person's wants and needs and demonstration of the links between a person's mood and events.

Supportive therapy, which has increasingly attracted research attention as 'a treatment package' in its own right, is being used in a variety of settings including general hospitals and primary care. It focuses on improving communication, encouraging ventilation of distress and building a therapeutic alliance through reassurance, problem-solving and instilling hope and optimism. These generic skills can be used by many frontline professionals at primary care level, with the provider helping the client to recognise feelings such as guilt, anxiety and anger alongside their usual response patterns. Referral on may be necessary, however, where it is felt that the older person's needs are more complex.

Other therapy approaches
Narrative therapy
In my experience, a neglected and under-appreciated group of therapists are those who practise using a narrative therapy model. Narration of a life story has the potential to secure a person's legacy and allow other practitioners to understand the individual behind the illness. This form of counselling is quite empowering, as it separates people from their problems and challenges that they are grappling with and shows them how, as experts in their own lives, they can uncover the dreams, values, goals and skills that truly define their identity. These are the buried stories that can be rewritten and incorporated into their story of the future. Human Givens therapists (see below) incorporate this kind of work into their practice.

Human Givens therapy
Human Givens interventions are typically short, making it one of the most cost- and time-effective interventions available in the therapy landscape. Therapists work with clients to set their own realistic goals, give useful psychoeducation (for example to explain what is happening when unpleasant psychological

symptoms are experienced in a way that removes the fear), obtain regular client feedback on progress and work to achieve effective, rapid change within the quickest timeframe. A Human Givens approach combines the best of solution-focused, cognitive-behavioural, narrative and person-centred approaches, all within a framework of identifying what important needs are not being met or resources unintentionally being misused, and addressing that. In couples therapy from this perspective, the focus is on finding ways that both parties' emotional needs are healthily met.

Reminiscence therapy
Reminiscence therapy can take many forms and is essentially the process of helping an older person who is struggling with memory to recall the remote past, with the aim of resocialising and making relationships. Reminiscence is often done in group settings, where group members can make new friends, learn communication skills and share feelings, improve self-esteem and validate each other's life experiences and struggles. It can be conducted in a variety of settings, including nursing and care homes.

Family therapy
Family therapists stress the importance of the wider family system with all its inherent rules and assumptions that govern the actions of those within it. They will work with as many members of the family as possible to resolve conflicts and promote better understanding of each other.

Psychodynamic therapy
Evolved from Freud's theory of the unconscious, this therapy concentrates on guiding clients to become aware of unconscious long-standing conflicts from the past which may

be impinging on today. It takes the stance that hidden mental processes account for many personal troubles experienced. The idea is that, with these new 'insights', clients will be able to find ways of doing things differently. (Proviso: Psychodynamic therapy can take years and, although people do claim new insights, many don't easily find more positive, less stressful ways of living as a result.)

Person-centred therapy

All therapies should be client-centred, of course, but the person-centred approach focuses on letting clients take the lead so that eventually they will arrive at their own understandings and solutions. The therapist remains non-directive and non-judgemental, and does not interrupt or give advice; they may ask for clarification or more detail only about specifics that the client raises. (Proviso: The difficulty may be that, when a person is emotionally overwhelmed – as very many are, when seeking therapy – this floods their ability to think straight, let alone creatively, and so clients may sometimes end up going round and round in circles.)

Couples therapy

It is wrong to assume that all is always well in the marital garden of older adults just because both parties still continue to live under the same roof in varying degrees of harmony. Couples therapy can be indicated for people who suddenly find themselves disenchanted and dissatisfied at spending much more time together because of retirement. A skilled marital therapist can help craft a different path for both parties, advocating a blend of 'together time' and private time to explore and develop separate interests.

Some people come to realise in later life that they are looking in vain for qualities in their partner that don't exist anymore, or have never existed in the first place. Marital therapy in these situations may help achieve the fairest and best parting of ways, whilst time still allows for either or both parties to form other relationships and friendships.

Bereavement therapy
Bereavement or grief therapy is rightly to be considered an important psychological intervention for older people, who are much more likely than younger people to go through often multiple bereavements. But it must be stressed that even a severe and acute emotional reaction to grief is not necessarily a pathological event. The reality is that older people are remarkably stoical and do adapt to serial losses in the form of witnessing the passing away of siblings, spouses, friends and even occasionally their adult children, displaying remarkable levels of resilience in the face of these losses.

For many, of course, the primary loss is the loss of a partner or spouse who has been a lifelong companion and trusted friend – the warmer and more supportive the relationship, the more persistent the grief is likely to be once the other person has departed. Grief is experienced both physically and psychologically, and people in grief often cry easily, have trouble sleeping, express little interest in food, have difficulty concentrating, and may not be able to make sound decisions. The ill health that may be a consequence of grief and bereavement may possibly be due to a stress-related, detrimental impact on the immune system. However, health setbacks are not inevitable, as adjustment eventually occurs. We should be mindful that, although grief is a severe reaction to a potentially overwhelming setback in life, for the vast majority it is a self-limiting condition, not a permanent state. In my experience, intense grieving rarely persists beyond one or two years after the passing away of a loved one.

The primary focus of grief therapy may initially be an empathic caring response, but active guidance to allow the bereaved person to accept the reality of the loss, as well as experience and process its pain, may be necessary. Finding an enduring connection to the lost person that allows the person to commit to the future without disrespecting the memory of the deceased is crucial. These are examples of the intricate, delicately balanced parallel tasks involved in helping the bereaved.

Therapy is often conducted individually or in a group context by specialist volunteers. (Proviso: the person-centred approach is the one most commonly used.) Looking out for signs such as suicidal thinking, severe weight loss, delusional thinking or severely impaired concentration and functioning is very important if the bereaved person is to receive the correct level of care. For some, a simple therapeutic focus on learning new coping skills in relation to tasks and chores that their deceased partner hitherto carried out, or ways to handle loneliness, social situations and anniversaries is a vital part of maintaining independence and fighting through sorrow.

Group therapy

Group therapy is very often offered in outpatient settings for people with depression. Considering older people for inclusion in a closed therapy group should be carried out carefully, and with due deliberation and caution. Many older people will have had lots of experience with group activities through day centres, active retirement groups and other community-based interventions, and will be relatively comfortable with them; others, however, may not have participated in group events since their schooldays and may find a group extremely daunting. Delivering therapy in a group setting may seem cost effective, but older people's preferences for individual work should not be set aside just to cut therapy waiting lists.

While older people may derive a great sense of satisfaction and belonging from participating in a group, mutually agreed ground rules and even formalised policies (covering issues such as confidentiality) need to be clearly articulated and discussed at the outset in order to ensure that group members feel safe in expressing their feelings and that group participation is relevant and meaningful.

Provision also needs to be made for those with mobility or sensory impairments; technology, such as the use of electronic hearing devices, can have a vital role to play in maximising group attendance and participation.

Well-run groups can offer peer support and provide a forum for improving self-esteem and self-understanding. They may offer not only companionship but also activity and can very effectively demonstrate that other people are grappling with similar problems to our own. Such groups may, therefore, also foster a sense of altruism in participants who, in addition to benefiting from the experience themselves, have the opportunity to help each other.

How to choose a therapist

There is much evidence now that our brains are more capable of growth and regeneration than we ever used to think possible. It is not so much that we lose our former selves as we age but that, like the trunk of a tree, more 'layers' get added with the passing years, in the form of mental attributes and resources and rich life experiences. The perspective of age also can bestow an emotional freedom, as the inessentials of life get sloughed off and increased psychological maturity helps us resolve many issues that perplexed and vexed us when we were young.

We do run into inevitable turbulence from time to time, however, as we are buffeted by bereavements, sickness and other losses. Whilst most life veterans manage these transitions and challenges with resilience, resourcefulness and hardiness, others may welcome assistance in the form of appropriate therapy from time to time to help them navigate the occasional storm. For those who jealously safeguard their mental health and who seek to have the very best therapy to restore the significant asset that is mental well-being, the following checklist will be useful:

An effective psychotherapist will:
- understand the different ways depression may present in later life and show how to lift you out of this state
- provide immediate help with anxiety in any of its forms, including trauma, phobias, panic attacks and obsessive compulsive behaviour
- have a range of skills to break the cycle of addictive behaviour
- give advice and their professional point of view if asked to do so
- avoid using technical jargon
- not dwell on past experiences which may have little if any connection with current difficulties
- be supportive when difficult feelings emerge, but without encouraging you to remain in an emotionally upset state
- know how to help you develop social skills which may have become impaired by isolation, loss of confidence and emotional distress. This will ensure that human needs for affection, friendship, pleasure, intimacy, connection to a wider network and community can be met
- activate and draw on your own resources, which may be much greater than you realise
- be mindful of the effects of therapy on the people who are close to the person being counselled

- help you to detach yourself from your problems and concerns, and to see them in a new and empowering way
- be able to use a wide range of appropriate techniques and skills, including the skill of deep relaxation; explaining, demonstrating and practising them as necessary
- set out and fully explain any practice to be done in between sessions
- increase self-agency and independence, and ensure that you feel better and more informed after every session attended
- achieve a positive outcome in therapy in as few sessions as possible. (Therapies that require at least ten sessions – and some may go on for years – can lead to dependency on the therapist and a reduced sense of client self-efficacy in the longer term.)

A trustworthy therapist will also:
- respect confidentiality and any limits that may apply to this, in case of risk to you or anyone else
- be explicit about costs of therapy
- know when to refer a client on to another professional if sufficient progress is not being made with your case
- be able to demonstrate that they belong to an appropriate professional or regulatory body to maintain competence, a code of conduct and supervisory arrangements
- be willing to work with any person irrespective of gender, age, racial or ethnic background and, where the therapist is unfamiliar with cultural factors impinging on a particular problem, indicate a willingness to become informed about these issues outside the session time
- be honest in declaring any particular area of expertise or sub-specialism or relevant areas where the therapist is *not* experienced in the management of a particular issue

- maintain accurate records of consultations, to be shared with the client upon request
- advocate with any other agency or organisation that the client requests and communicate with any other professionals that the client may wish their therapist to be in contact with
- have a policy for dealing with any unsolicited contact from friends or family members of the client which preserves confidentiality but allows emergency contact to be made in special circumstances, such as an emergency involving risk to the client or anyone else
- be willing to meet with supporters or family members for purposes of information gathering and to explain, reassure and encourage persistence with therapy, if asked by the client to do so
- have sufficient spare emotional capacity to work with the client (i.e. not be distracted by their own concerns).

It has to be borne in mind, however, that the cost of private therapy, while often a barrier for all age groups, may particularly be so for older people, who may have to rely on fixed incomes. Not only is there the cost of the therapy itself, but there are also likely to be transport costs incurred in getting to and from the venue. Even when people are fortunate enough to possess private health insurance, the companies may be reluctant to reimburse the cost of psychological treatment fully – or even partially. Publicly funded therapy, on the other hand, may be of variable quality and beset by long waiting lists.

If you do decide to try private treatment, but it will be a struggle to pay the full fee, do broach the issue of cost at the outset, as frequently a discount or a sliding scale of fees can be made available in circumstances of hardship. Most therapists understand financial imperatives and are not professionally affronted by discussion of cost.

Specific therapy skills when working with the older person

A good therapist will:

- carry out careful assessment of the client, looking out for memory and cognitive issues. Physical illness can influence presentations of many psychological symptoms. Therapy in certain circumstances, therefore, may initially need to be conducted in collaboration with an older person's medical advisor, to be certain that any medical issues are not contributing to the mental health of the client.

- want to be aware of and, to a degree, informed about the history that is influential in an older person's life story – the global civil rights movement, for example, or the Cold War. The life story of each individual older person is, from a Human Givens perspective, a template for successful therapy and will often reveal hidden examples of resilience and healing from earlier years. Older people are nothing if not resilient and their continued existence and survival is implicit proof of this, even when inner resources appear temporarily blunted by severe depression.

- be comfortable dealing with issues surrounding death and dying. Acknowledgement of the contribution of caregiver stress and the coping ability or otherwise of significant others may require a practical, problem-solving approach to defusing the stress associated with the care of more dependent older adults.

- take into account the norms of the environment from which the client hails. Some clients will live in institutional settings, others may reside in age-segregated communities and it is important to learn the social rules of each.

- know to move to more neutral ground, if the older client is initially reluctant to open-up in therapy. They might raise something significant or interesting in the news or ask a question that encourages the person to use their longer-term memory and recount a story as indirect means of starting to glean a sense of priorities and concerns.
- be aware of services available for older adults, including the voluntary sector. Being able to recommend these with confidence to clients may make as significant a practical difference to quality of life as successful therapy.

Therapy amidst cognitive decline

Whilst some progress has been achieved in challenging the therapeutic pessimism that has surrounded the area of psychological therapy for older people in general, the role of psychotherapy in dementia is poorly understood and under-researched. A diagnosis of Alzheimer's disease, which is the top cause of the dementia syndrome, can have serious personal and social implications, yet despite the limitations of medical and drug treatments and the need for care and support of sufferer and carer alike, for many therapists it is an illness entirely outside the comfort zone of their training and practice. The tasks to be worked through in therapy are significant, from accepting and coping with the initial diagnosis to devising strategies to deal with behavioural disturbance later in the condition. Although challenging behaviours are commonplace with dementia and cognitive decline, they are by no means inevitable and there is no single trajectory of deterioration that clients and families can anticipate and prepare for. For some, dementia may be a relatively benign condition, and the therapy focus may best be on strategies to make the most out of the cognitive abilities that are preserved and maintained.

Human Givens therapists place special emphasis on clients' life stories as from these will emerge resources, talents and attributes, the deployment of which can be used to overcome many problems and challenges in that person's life. In the case of dementia, building a narrative, story or subjective account of the person's life early on in the condition is crucial, otherwise memories may be lost as the illness progresses – not every person has a family member to fill in the gaps of a person's biography. The story may even help the person's professional carers to see beyond the illness and to put many of their behaviours in a human context.

For those with milder age-related cognitive impairment, increasing environmental and social stimulation can halt or reverse age-associated intellectual decline. Therapists need to remind their clients that our brains are much more plastic or 'acrobatic' than previously believed, and that even in late old age we are capable of learning new skills, if given sufficient time and training. Some clients benefit from support in coping with depressive symptoms that accompany a diagnosis of dementia, when insight and awareness of the condition is not yet lost or impaired. Special models of cognitive behavioural therapy (CBT), interpersonal therapy, structured counselling and behavioural activation have been developed to reduce depression in dementia.

Clients who have more established cognitive deficits may benefit from therapies such as reality orientation or cognitive stimulation therapy, to help them challenge disorientation and to reconnect with their present environment, as well as their past, by activating retained knowledge and experience. As well as plenty of informal reminders such as labelling of rooms, cupboards and drawers, noticeboards and highly visible calendars, reminiscence can also be a useful tool here, perhaps packaged as exercises for a group setting 'to bring people up to date' – such as by discussing current affairs and newspaper articles and drawing comparisons between present day events and historical incidents.

In general, accepting the confused person's subjective experience as valid, even if their expressed experiences are flavoured by disorientation, is important. Even as dementia enters its latter stages, playing to the person's strengths by tapping into their long-term memory and referring to events from the past, rather than endlessly hoping to orientate them to the present, can improve morale and mood in no small way. Seeing meaning in all behaviour is very helpful whenever a care situation becomes difficult or when a range of problematic behaviours present themselves, such as aggression, agitation, dis-inhibition, etc. Skill in interpreting underlying issues underpinning emotional/behavioural upset, such as a change or disruption in routine, is invaluable and especially relevant when the person with dementia has language difficulties and can no longer express this for themselves. It is important to reinforce that the behaviour is a product of illness and is not wilfully produced.

Key needs at this time are for security (which includes arranging individuals' living environments in ways that help them orientate themselves and have maximum awareness of their surroundings); attention (including the sensitive and intuitive interpretation of behavioural and emotional disturbances); status (affirming in every way possible that people still have a value and reminding them of all that they used to value about themselves); stimulation (a balance of novel experiences and long-loved pleasures); and comfort and affection. Therapy in the context of cognitive impairment and dementia is thus a skilful craft, as this population has particular needs which have been underserved by conventional care and treatment approaches to date.

Adapting therapy for older people

It is important for a therapist to recruit any ally, preferably nominated by the client, in the form of a friend or family member willing to support the therapy process. This can take the form of help with transport to and from the session, and waiting in between. Such practical support can make the difference between the treatment successfully getting off the ground or burning out on the launch pad at the start.

A treatment course of ten to twenty sessions may simply be too long for frail people with limited life expectancy. Equally, a session length of sixty to ninety minutes may be excessive for people with challenging sensory issues, such as deafness, or conditions that make it painful to sit or where frequent access to a toilet is needed. The session length may usefully be shortened to forty minutes, and there should be maximum flexibility around 'homework' or reflection that a client is asked to engage in between sessions.

The treatment goals must be realistic and respectful of individual circumstances.

The pace of therapy may need to be slower, taking into account, for instance, reduced speed of information processing.

Providing memory aids and summaries of sessions (with larger fonts) is a considerate and helpful way of encouraging assimilation of the material covered.

The therapist must also be aware of the commonly held beliefs, expectations of roles and gender and culturally held assumptions of some older clients and only confront these if it is necessary for progress on a specific aspect of treatment.

Therapists working with an older client group need to become familiar with age-specific stressors such as chronic illness and disability, loss of loved ones and the strain of their own care-giving responsibilities where relevant.

For those who lack reliable transportation or who have a disability or mobility impairment and who are already comfortable with, and adjusted to, receiving a whole range of personal care in the home, it may make sense to provide the therapy there too – although some therapists may feel vulnerable offering this domiciliary service. An alternative is phone or internet-based interventions, which may also help older adults overcome common therapy barriers and be less stigmatising to engage with. Many therapists will feel comfortable visiting residents in nursing or retirement homes.

While some adults may approach their 'golden years' with eager anticipation, looking forward to retirement, spending time with their grandchildren or simply wishing to savour a new phase of life, others may dread the physical and mental effects of the ageing process. The job of therapy is to help older adults who may have difficulty with ageing transitions to manage their emotions, find new sources of enjoyment and meaning and also new support systems. Ideally, therapy will not be shy about helping people face uncomfortable fears of death and dying, if they exist, and also deal with grief and loss.

We must also remember the potential benefit of support for caregivers of older people. It has been consistently reported that 50 per cent of carers of people with dementia experience depressive symptoms themselves, often due to carer burnout. Failure to support them can lead to a complete breakdown of often precarious care arrangements, as well as the premature placement of the older person in institutional care. Skilled therapy can open up communication issues within families to ensure appropriate burden sharing, discussion around delicate end-of-life care issues, finances and inheritance, and use of community resources and professional care to supplement family efforts.

Why Human Givens therapy is especially suitable for older adults

In my opinion, the most suitable form of therapy for older people is one that is relatively brief and focuses on setting and achieving goals, empowering a person in ways to meet them and monitoring progress. This is all part and parcel of the Human Givens approach. In a Human Givens session, the exact steps for achieving interim objectives are carefully mapped out, rehearsed and reviewed to gauge longer-term progress. Tracing the exact pathology of a symptom or problem may be fruitless in the extreme, whereas visualising change and being free of a given symptom or pattern of behaviour is powerfully re-moralising for the client, who feels their sense of agency improve exponentially.

Above all, with the evidence that significant behavioural change and benefits can occur in very few sessions (three out of four patients are symptom free or reliably improved in an average of only 3.6 sessions with a Human Givens therapist, superior to outcomes published for the UK government's IAPT programme, which mainly relies on a CBT-based model[3]), a Human Givens approach is in keeping with lives lived by even our oldest citizens, who don't have an over-abundance of time to spend on achieving therapeutic change and improving the quality of their lives.

How Human Givens therapy works

Using the framework of ensuring that people's emotional and psychological needs are optimally met and their innate resources being used effectively, the Human Givens approach integrates techniques from many tried-and-tested therapeutic

---

3   William P. Andrews et al., 'A Five-Year Evaluation of the Human Givens Therapy Using a Practice Research Network', *Mental Health Review Journal*, Vol. 18, No. 3 (2013), pp. 165–76.

approaches, blending them in the most effective way. The refreshingly down-to-earth, common-sense aspects of it may make it particularly appealing to no-nonsense older people.

Engaging in the therapy is fundamentally non-threatening for any older person who is initially reluctant to talk or who is new to the process of therapy in general because empathy and rapport building are at the core of Human Givens techniques. The ability to establish a safe and trusting rapport is the foundation for any therapeutic change and subsequent engagement in treatment and, for older people who may have felt dismissed and ignored by many other services and professionals, establishing rapport can be a vital dispeller of anxiety about the therapy process itself. Some other kinds of therapists, such as those more psychoanalytically trained or who exclusively use interpretive techniques, see any rapport building as virtually a boundary violation or certainly inappropriate behaviour, and insist on a sterile, neutral stance. Yet, in reality, rapport is fundamental to building trust and understanding, and therapy with an older person is likely to run into the ground without this crucial ingredient. The quality and detail of the narrative provided by the client will frequently rely on this foundation of a solid rapport.

A Human Givens therapist will help the client set an agenda for change, identifying specific goals to aim for and the resources already within the person that will help bring that change about. The therapist will provide different perspectives and also use humour, stories and various other creative ways to help people let go of disempowering patterns of thought and behaviour and adopt more life-enhancing new ones. An important part of the Human Givens armoury is psychoeducation, where the therapist will explain and normalise exactly why anxiety, depression and other mental difficulties occur, why symptoms take the form they do and what is happening in the brain. This leads to much more willing acceptance of strategies to manage psychological challenges.

An important and, indeed, highly enjoyable element of Human Givens therapy is the focus on relaxation. The therapist will demonstrate and teach simple breathing and visualisation techniques and give the client the opportunity to experience deep relaxation for themselves through a process called guided imagery (a guided relaxation). This will be an entirely novel experience for many older people, is totally non-threatening and the client remains aware and 'in charge' at all times.

On occasion, an older person may be so distressed, so shut down with depression, for instance, that it may almost seem dismissive and callous to invite them to relax. In my experience, I have rarely seen anyone forego this opportunity, even when they are entirely sceptical about the possibility of change or in denial about the extent of their difficulties. Most of will gladly seize the opportunity of at least brief respite. It is also not true that attempts to induce relaxation in an older person will promptly result in them falling asleep every time.

In guided imagery, the therapist usually invites the client to imagine being in a lovely, relaxing place in nature and guides them to experience it fully through all their senses. (Such a scene, if created in sufficient detail, can be a joyful place to return to mentally whenever practising relaxation alone or when someone is stressed or has difficulty sleeping.) When deep relaxation has been induced, the therapist will guide the client to imagine carrying out the goals they have set for themselves, remaining positive, calm and managing any minor setback. Guided imagery is, in effect, the doorway through which new learning passes, with appropriate metaphors and therapeutic suggestion enabling the emergence of new behaviours and perspectives, which embed most effectively when a person is in a deeply relaxed trance state. The clinical experience of Human Givens therapists indicates that more rapid therapeutic change occurs when using guided imagery than with any other technique used in therapy.

Most importantly, the Human Givens approach allows people to experience healing and change from the very first session, which powerfully instils hope and restores morale for many older people.

Human Givens therapy with older people

The following (anonymised) case histories illustrate how the Human Givens approach may be successfully applied in a variety of clinical settings, where older people present with different forms of emotional and psychological distress.

Neil, aged 68, attended therapy privately, on the recommendation of a friend, because of the low mood and anxiety he was experiencing. He had been married twice, with two adult children and one grandchild from his first marriage and a 12-year-old daughter from his second marriage. Sadly, both marriages had ended in acrimonious divorces but Neil was now in a new relationship. However, he had stopped engaging in activities he used to enjoy and had become quite incommunicative, which his partner, Annie, found frustrating. At her urging, Neil had seen his GP, who had prescribed antidepressant medication. This didn't especially help his low mood, unfortunately, but it did cause sexual difficulties, which had begun to strain his new relationship further.

'I'm just a burden on everyone,' Neil said at his first session, holding his head in his hands. 'Honestly, I think they would all be better off if I were dead.' It emerged that he blamed himself for the break-up of his two previous marriages, although he maintained a good relationship with his children, going to great lengths to keep up contact with all of them and never defaulting on his financial obligations.

During the ensuing discussion, he agreed that suicide wasn't the legacy he wished to leave his family and he responded to the therapist's suggestion that it would be a horribly permanent solution to what was actually temporary distress, which he could be quite quickly helped out of; he willingly went on to make a safety contract with his therapist, whereby he would talk with a friend if he felt extremely low and promised to reduce his drinking, which he had increased recently in an effort to drown his sorrows. He was also highly relieved to learn that his impotence was most likely down to his medication and resolved to seek advice from his GP about tapering down the medication. In these small ways, he was already encouraged to start feeling more hopeful for the future.

The therapist challenged Neil's black-and-white thinking about being unlovable, reminding him of how he was a loyal father and an excellent role model for his children, and that the ending of his two previous relationships were not all down to him. She explained to him that the more he withdrew from simple pleasures and activities, and the more he spent time alone dwelling on the past and castigating himself, the worse he would feel – and the more worrying and miserable that would be for those around him. This made sense to him and he was receptive to the idea that, to break the cycle, he had to engage in activities again, even if initially he didn't feel he wanted to.

So they discussed ways that he could bring back pleasure into his life and talked about what he used to enjoy. 'Annie and I used to love going out for a meal,' he said. He agreed to surprise her by arranging a meal out. As he had always liked golf, he also decided to go back to his golf club, thereby meeting his needs for attention, intimacy and being part of a wider community.

Neil appeared to benefit greatly from deep relaxation and guided imagery, during which his therapist was able to remind him of his many positive attributes. She decided to use the rewind technique (a non-invasive means of neutralising traumatic memories while deeply relaxed) to deal with the heightened emotions still surrounding the break-up of his first marriage, which particularly troubled him. Afterwards, she guided him to visualise enjoying his new relationship with Annie again.

At the second session Neil reported an enjoyable night out with Annie and particularly commented on the benefits that golf had brought him in lowering his distress; the therapist encouraged him to enter the veterans' four-ball golf tournament that he had mentioned, to boost his sense of achievement and competence. By the third and final session Neil was reporting a considerable improvement in mood and had joined a yoga class with Annie, which provided them with a shared interest. It was also a place where Neil could practise the relaxation exercises that he had made part of his daily routine.

. . .

John and Pat, both aged 72, came to therapy to discuss a significant change in their family dynamics. Both had been retired for ten years and had initially greatly enjoyed this new chapter in their lives, as they were comfortably off. However, their elder son Andrew, aged 41, had recently returned to live in the family home after the breakdown of his marriage. He was in a troubled mental state, resulting in the atmosphere at home becoming very strained. Andrew had also started drinking quite heavily and, as a result of incapacitating hangovers, had routinely been arriving late for work. The upshot of this was that he had been moved to a zero-hours contract by his employer, and so was struggling to pay any maintenance to his ex-wife and three children.

John and Pat were in a state of considerable distress, both about what had happened to Andrew and the impact it was having on his children and on their own health and well-being. 'There seems to be no end in sight,' said Pat. Andrew had given his parents no indication of when he intended to move out and saw no need to contribute anything to the household bills. 'We must have done something very wrong when we brought him up,' she said, 'otherwise surely he would be able to stand on his own two feet.'

John, meanwhile, had become very concerned about the effect of Andrew's behaviour on Pat, but felt intimidated by his son at times, saying, 'I don't want to say or do anything that might push him over the edge'.

The Human Givens therapist made a point of telling John and Pat that their dilemma was far from unique, to normalise their distress. Largely because of spiralling housing costs and poor job security, a quarter of young adults in the UK still live with their parents, which is a record number. The 'boomerang' effect, she pointed out, was not because John and Pat did not parent their son sufficiently well to make him 'stand on his own two feet', but rather reflected difficult and challenging circumstances in his life which were a consequence of his independence, not dependence.

The therapist allowed John and Pat to express their concerns for Andrew's children, caught in the middle of the break-up, and Pat's hurt that Andrew chose to have his 'access time' with them away from the house. Then together they explored John and Pat's understandable instinct to try to 'fix' everything for Andrew, while simultaneously feeling taken advantage of. The therapist helped them to see the negative outcomes of giving Andrew free rein in the house, in that it was adding to his parents' frustrations. She explained the importance of recognising the meeting of their own emotional needs as individuals and as a couple – the danger of allowing Andrew to dominate their every conversation was becoming a setback to the freedom and closeness that they had enjoyed since retirement. She also taught them the skills of relaxation and visualisation, demonstrating the techniques with each of them.

It was agreed that they should treat Andrew as an independent adult, despite his setbacks, and John was given the support and strength to initiate a conversation with Andrew. They decided that drawing up a contract, as one would with a lodger, would be the best way forward. Pat initially felt that treating Andrew even as a 'lodger with love' was harsh, but she came to agree that it was better to be clear about the house rules that needed respecting and how much Andrew would be expected to pay for household costs. This would probably make him feel less guilty, too, about imposing on his parents at his age.

After discussion, Pat also decided to encourage Andrew to bring his children over to the house during his access visits by offering a mini-celebration party for her grandchildren to enjoy every week.

Their next session was their last, as they didn't feel the need for further help afterwards. They reported that Andrew had been receptive to their conversation and the atmosphere had improved immeasurably. He had started to drink a little less, even if just because he had to save some money for his household contribution, and found he enjoyed spending time with his children and their grandparents together, rather than trying to assert what remained of his independence by seeing them apart. Pat also reported that she had successfully resisted the urge to cook and clean clothes for Andrew, feeling a much greater sense of her own autonomy as a result, and had even managed to persuade him to see a therapist himself, to begin the process of his own personal healing.

. . .

Doris, 82, lived in a local authority nursing home. She had been a widow for many years but had remained independent until painful arthritis obliged her to move to a nursing home six months previously. Her two adult sons both lived about sixty miles away, visited relatively infrequently and often forgot to call. She had become much more uncommunicative and withdrawn in recent weeks, and care attendants in the nursing home were concerned about her growing confused state in the evenings.

The GP who visited the home didn't believe there was any reason for Doris to be depressed; after all, she had settled into the home initially very well and appeared to be well looked after. However, as he was aware of the Human Givens approach and knew a therapist who would be willing to visit the nursing home, he wished to 'cover himself' by having Doris assessed by her, in case either of Doris' two sons called him to enquire after her.

The therapist agreed to assess Doris at the nursing home, although she had a policy of always offering an office-based consultation as an alternative, in case a client might wish to talk about day-to-day care issues and feel less free to do this in the setting of the nursing home itself. Before accepting the referral, the therapist, who had previously been a nurse, asked the staff to run a full set of blood tests and to take a urine sample to exclude urinary tract infection, which could have caused or added to her difficulties. No concerns were thrown up by the results.

The therapist at once recognised many symptoms of clinical depression in Doris. She felt that the poor concentration and sense of slowed mental reaction, combined with anxiety over relatively minor issues, were the tell-tale, if not classic, signs of low mood in this age group. She wondered about the cumulative effects of loneliness, pain from Doris' arthritis and the presence of cognitive decline, made worse by the lack of stimulation in the nursing home. The arthritis pains, coupled with stiffness, had reduced Doris' mobility significantly, leaving her choosing to stay isolated in her room, as she was terrified of falling.

Having established which of Doris' key emotional needs were absent or difficult for her to obtain in her present surroundings, the therapist spoke to the staff in the facility and encouraged them to take Doris out to an active retirement group near to the nursing home, so that Doris could meet some of her former neighbours. She also spoke to one of Doris' sons and asked them to initiate more phone calls to their mother and to bring in some personal belongings from Doris' old home to her room in the nursing home. This gave Doris a great deal of pleasure.

Doris was also encouraged to become involved in creative pursuits in the home, in particular the painting class, as painting had previously given her pleasure. Doris became better able to concentrate on relaxation and was guided to imagine for herself a soothing light beamed onto her sore joints. She was also encouraged to distract herself from her arthritis pains by paying close attention to her surroundings – for instance, setting herself the task of noticing every little change in the tree outside her window, with the passing seasons.

The therapist strengthened Doris's sense of identity and self-esteem by asking lots of questions about her life as a teacher before she married, then focusing on her life as a wife, friend and mother to her two sons. Doris eagerly took up the therapist's offer to record segments of her life story and compile it, along with photos, in an album to be left as a legacy for her grandchildren and great-grandchildren, who visited her a few times a year. Gradually, Doris improved in mood, appeared less disoriented and confused, and began to enjoy and participate more in the routine of the home.

. . .

Sheila, 66, had begun to experience episodes of panic and anxiety with insomnia. She was the main caregiver for her 70-year-old husband, who had dementia, and was also intimately involved in the care of her 92-year-old mother, who still lived independently. Sheila had fears about how she would cope when her mother passed away and had nightmares about being at her mother's funeral and breaking down while reading a eulogy for her. Although she had been offered two weeks of respite care for her husband in a local nursing home, which she would have welcomed, her husband had refused to go – 'I'm reluctant to put too much pressure on him to accept, as he made me promise never to put him in a nursing home,' she said to her Human Givens therapist.

Sheila had come to see the therapist on the advice of her GP, after he declined to issue her a second course of sleeping tablets for fear of inducing a dependency on them. The therapist took a detailed account of the triggers for Sheila's panic episodes as well as noting any symptoms of depression that might be an underlying driver of her distress. In her role as caregiver for two people, Sheila had essentially given up all outside interests, including membership of a book club and weekly attendance at a choir, which she had loved being part of. She felt guilty about taking any time off and had recently refused an offer from her daughter of a weekend away, as she felt it would be unfair to leave John, even though her other daughter was prepared to stay with him. 'He won't like her doing the intimate things, you know ...'

The therapist explained to Sheila how the brain works in anxiety and depression – innate needs not being met leaving Sheila increasingly aroused and anxious, and the excessive worrying interfering with sleep and leading her to have more dreams and nightmares. All this had led, in turn, to her physical exhaustion and depression.

Sheila was encouraged to find ways to set time aside for herself and to practise visualisation – getting up ten minutes earlier every day to enjoy her 'private time' – and to develop better sleep strategies through setting a fixed time for waking and going to bed. In guided imagery, the therapist used metaphor to reframe the content of Sheila's dreams and, as Sheila considered herself spiritual, suggested that the death of her mother, at some point in the future, would be a natural re-birthing into the next world, and that the 'worn-out overcoat' that is our bodily form would be exchanged for a spiritual form that saw us freed from the physical limitations of ageing. Sheila was led to visualise herself reading the most moving tribute to her mother at her future funeral service whilst being calm and composed, but also giving herself permission to allow any emotion to come to the surface which would be entirely appropriate and indeed even congruent with the occasion.

Education from the therapist about 'burnout' and the so-called 'carer syndrome' was especially interesting to Sheila. Unrelieved caring for a person with a chronic illness can result in exhaustion, rage, anger or guilt. Sheila was urged to be more compassionate to herself and more mindful of the reality that being a carer is one of the most difficult jobs there is. She was also encouraged to accept more support, offered by her adult children, in caring for John, which enabled her to engage again, even if irregularly, with her book group and choir. She also agreed to allow her children to raise with their father the matter of the two-week respite in the nursing home, to persuade him that Sheila badly needed a break. Addressing all these factors in therapy helped Sheila considerably.

· · ·

Tom, a 74-year-old widower, had recently been diagnosed with early prostate cancer. He lived alone and, when he attended his GP surgery for a routine check, his GP noticed that he seemed very withdrawn and had lost a considerable amount of weight. The GP requested an assessment from a Human Givens therapist, as he wondered if there were issues that were unresolved in relation to the death of his wife eighteen months earlier.

The therapist established that, despite Tom's favourable prognosis – the cancer having been discovered at an early stage – he still tended to disbelieve the specialists, who he felt were 'fobbing me off' whenever he asked about the need for repeat tumour marker blood tests. There was no evidence of pathological grief, such as excessive guilt, bottling up emotions about his wife's death, denial of her passing or signs of post-traumatic stress. Indeed, Tom and his wife had enjoyed a close relationship and, although he missed her enormously, he had seemed to be grieving appropriately.

Tom admitted he felt completely hopeless for the future, however, and had withdrawn from a lot of the activities that had provided him and his wife with meaning and purpose. He had been having suicidal thoughts and even discussed the means by which he had contemplated ending his life – 'I've still got my wife's medication. That was only because I forgot to clear it away with her other stuff at the time, but now I see it as my insurance policy, you know, in case I can't carry on.' More worryingly, he had visited the family solicitor the previous week to update his will and, to the surprise of his daughter, who was very close to him, had recently given away a family heirloom, which was uncharacteristic of him.

Tom's therapist referred him back to his GP after the first consultation, with specific queries as to whether Tom was now so depressed that he could benefit from medication and whether he needed a safer environment (i.e. acute admission to his local psychiatric facility), in view of the fact that his daughter was away at the time. The therapist acted correctly in referring Tom back to his GP because, while there is much concern about increasing rates of suicide amongst adolescents and young people, the suicide rate amongst older people remains stubbornly high. In many respects, Tom presented with the 'classic' combination of risk factors for those who go on to kill themselves, including being widowed, male and having both a potentially serious physical illness and depression.

The GP didn't feel that Tom needed hospital admission but started him on an antidepressant in conjunction with the antipsychotic olanzapine to reduce anxiety and to improve sleep and appetite. With Tom's consent, contact with Tom's daughter was also made on her return to explain the perceived increase in his level of risk with a view to mobilising and increasing the level of support available to him from family.

Tom seemed to improve quite quickly but became concerned about the side effects of olanzapine, which increased his appetite and caused weight gain. His GP gradually discontinued this drug and Tom made another appointment to see his therapist, who continued to check in with him about suicidal thoughts, even in the face of Tom's apparent improvement. It is known that, before any psychological improvement occurs, antidepressants lessen the physical symptoms of depression, such as lack of motivation, so suicidal risk may temporarily *increase* after starting medication because the person may have more energy to act on the suicidal thoughts.

Therapy with Tom involved lowering his emotional arousal levels and setting goals to help him re-engage with activities and community supports. He came to accept that he had made a good recovery from his cancer, finding guided imagery of visualising his immune system winning a battle with cancer cells especially useful. He was encouraged to construct a new image of himself as someone who was both mentally and physically tough and resilient, despite the challenge of cancer. Tom ultimately responded very well to the joint efforts of his therapist and GP, and came to see his recovery as a second chance at life. He exercised much more and became a more hands-on grandparent and father, drawing strength from and strengthening the relationships that had protected him, provided him with meaning and prevented him from acting on the darkest depressive impulses.

The abundant gifts of later life: benefits restated

A new awareness of the needs of our most rapidly expanding segment of society is slowly emerging – we can no longer dismiss older people as irrelevant or invisible in an increasingly busy world. Older people have valuable contributions to make in enriching the communities and wider landscape they have shaped and can help recalibrate the priorities of a society in which interpersonal communication is under threat, where consumption is at an all-time high yet personal satisfaction and meaning are at an all-time low.

While no single magic bullet exists for the ills of the present era that erode our mental well-being, older people have the insight, wisdom and life experience to accept necessary change but also to temper it and to help 'future-proof' the next generation by showing how to make ambitions and aspirations sustainable, based on long-term needs rather than immediate wants.

Ageing can even be viewed as an accelerated series of opportunities to gain psychological and spiritual maturity.

The world needs to rid itself of bitterness, rivalry and vanity, and perhaps only elders can fully demonstrate the values of respect, compassion and tolerance – therefore the challenge and the priority for older people must be to remain enthusiastically engaged in as many aspects of life as possible; and not just to reflect with wisdom but also actively to share their perceptions and experience.

I look forward to when this wise generation begins confidently to realise the extent of the gifts they have to offer and don't doubt themselves simply because they have acquired grey hairs or developed a few extra furrows along their brows. But the value of advice and wise words from older people is determined not only by its intrinsic value and truth but also by the degree of empathy that the younger recipient shows towards the older sage. If younger people recognise that wiser elders are not seeking reimbursement but give advice and counsel purely out of love, then a personal connection occurs; the effect of the advice can be multiplied, and meaningful and mutually beneficial intergenerational communication begins. The wise younger person will continue to draw from the wisdom and lifetime of experience of older people, even when they begin to need care and support, enabling a meaningful relationship to continue for both.

Dogged optimism: how the future might look

If the trend towards increased life expectancy continues and as institutionalised retirement fades into history, people will have greater choice in terms of working into their eighties and beyond, if they wish to, working part-time, adopting a new career or retiring if financially feasible and desirable, but the hitherto brutal cut-off that was often enforced and mandatory on one's sixty-fifth birthday will likely go the way of the dodo. For those who do withdraw from the workplace, 'new leisure' will be ever more structured and allow us time to study, travel, up-skill, express ourselves creatively, seek new challenges or to simply take greater care of our health.

Treating older people as a group to be discriminated against will be outlawed, as will ageism in all its forms, and advertising directed at older people will no longer be patronising. Indeed, more products than ever will be adapted to the needs of older people, from furniture to cars and from packaging to technology.

Older people will still continue to bank most of the nation's finances, but will be called upon more than ever before to transfer assets to younger people, as their children will, alas, increasingly find housing and other services unaffordable. Nonetheless, more corporate and public power structures will be created with greater numbers of older people at the helm.

Rapid medical advances will stem the tide of premature mortality from illnesses such as cancer and heart disease and more treatments to stem the destruction of dementia will be available, so older people will remain more independent than ever before.

Long-term institutional care will be considered only after all attempts at supported or semi-independent living and home adaptation have been exhausted. Care environments will fulfil not only medical and nursing care needs but needs for recreation, social interaction and stimulation, with individually tailored lifestyle plans being as important as a medical prescription.

Political leaders will agree to fund continuing care, when needed, without older people having to liquidate their assets. Chronic illness may still exist but new drug therapies will manage symptoms more effectively and surgical treatment will become less invasive through keyhole techniques and more sophisticated scans. Modern technology will roll back physical constraints such as mobility impairments, leading to greater societal involvement by older people with physical disabilities.

The population as a whole will be encouraged to take a much wider view of prospects across the entire lifespan, and there will be greater versatility in society, with routine employment of older people as teachers and mentors in every walk of life, as wisdom and experience become more highly valued.

Age will set the political agenda and age-friendly cities, with adequate facilities and services, will become the norm, with acknowledgement from wider society that they contain benefit for everyone.

A charter of equal and mutual rights based on Human Givens principles will ensure that all societal frameworks, be they legal, political or economic, will be more in tune with human needs. Only this approach can foster the fluidity and flexibility to allow the full participation in society by its oldest members.

I truly believe that the beautiful minds of older people have bountiful gifts to share and the overlap between sustainable and meaningful living and mental health is significant. Ageing well through meeting key emotional needs at every stage in life should be the primary goal of every individual, family and society.

Contributors

DR MOLLY BREDIN is a higher specialist trainee in general adult psychiatry, currently working in liaison psychiatry. Having graduated from Trinity College Dublin in 2013, she commenced psychiatric training in 2014 and is a member of the College of Psychiatrists of Ireland and the Royal College of Psychiatrists. Dr Bredin's special interests include medical psychotherapy, anxiety and personality.

DR AILBHE DOHERTY is a specialist trainee in psychiatry currently working in the psychiatry of later life. Drawing from her degree in psychology, she believes strongly in promoting psychological resilience in older adults. Her research interests include mental health in doctors and the topic of suicidality. Dr Doherty is passionate about music and holds a diploma in violin performance from the Associated Board of the Royal School of Music.

DR JENNIFER KEANE is a higher specialist trainee in child and adolescent psychiatry currently working with services in the West of Ireland. She completed her basic specialist training in Dublin in 2018 and is a member of the College of Psychiatrists of Ireland and the Royal College of Psychiatrists. Dr Keane has a special interest in developmental trauma and the classification of mental disorders and is completing a master's degree in public health.